MW00454467

DRINKING WITH YOUR PATRON SAINTS

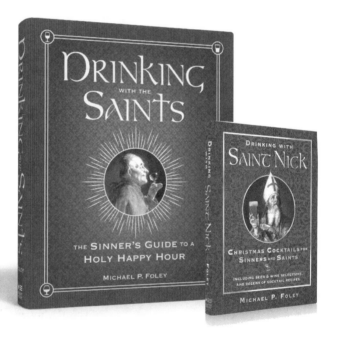

DRINKING WITH YOUR

Patron Saints

THE SINNER'S GUIDE TO HONORING NAMESAKES AND PROTECTORS

MICHAEL P. FOLEY

REGNERY
HISTORY

Regnery History™ is a trademark of Salem Communications Holding Corporation
Regnery® is a registered trademark of Salem Communications Holding Corporation

ISBN 978-1-68451-047-4
ebook ISBN 978-1-68451-066-5
LCCN 2019955219

Published in the United States by
Regnery History, an imprint of
Regnery Publishing
A Division of Salem Media Group
300 New Jersey Ave NW
Washington, DC 20001
www.Regnery.com

Manufactured in the United States of America

10 9 8 7 6 5 4 3 2 1

Books are available in quantity for promotional or premium use. For information on discounts and terms, please visit our website: www. Regnery.com.

O heavenly Patron, in whose name I glory, pray ever to God for me. Strengthen me in my faith; establish me in virtue; guard me in the conflict; that I may vanquish the malign foe and attain to everlasting glory. Amen.

—*The Raccolta*, no. 581

To all my patrons, both earthly and heavenly,
this book is gratefully dedicated

CONTENTS

INTRODUCTION

WHY THIS BOOK

One of the things that became obvious after the publication of *Drinking with the Saints* (2015) and *Drinking with Saint Nick* (2018) was the need for more like them. Readers across the country began using these books to enhance their celebrations throughout the year with a dose of good Christian cheer. And many, I was gratified to learn, benefited as much from the stories of the saints as they did from the drink ideas.

But even those lengthy treatments did not and could not include everything. Hence this sequel, or chaser if you will, which you now hold in your hands. Drawing from the resources of our earlier works and then some, *Drinking with Your Patron Saints* equips you with all you need to celebrate the rich heritage of patron saints.

THE PATRON SAINTS

Patron saints are almost as old as Christianity itself, but they are easily misunderstood. It is tempting to think of them as "replacements" of the Roman gods, in a sort of watered-down monotheism for recovering polytheists. This theory has the right location but the wrong causation. It was not the Roman pantheon but the Roman patron-client relationship that served as the inspiration for saintly patronage. In this important relationship, the client owed the patron honor and gifts while the patron owed the client certain favors, such as helping him find a job. Think of it as a legal and moral version of *The Godfather* movies, with all the big fat Italian weddings and without all the sleeping with the fishes.

Patron saints were initially reserved to the names of Christian churches, but over time they spread to all aspects of life: one's country, occupation, hobbies, illnesses, and dangers. Spiritually speaking, the point was not an alternative to God but a heavenly patron who could put in a good word for you and help you draw closer to God. For just as we turn to our friends on earth and ask for their help and prayers, we do the same with our friends snuggling in the Bosom of Abraham. Behind the idea of patron saints is the reassuring doctrine found in the Apostles' Creed: "the communion of saints." Because those who die in Christ do not really die but live in Him, there is a spiritual bond between the members of Christ's Mystical Body on Earth, in Heaven, and in Purgatory that neither death, disaster, nor devil can break.

How does a saint become a patron of a particular type of person, place, or thing? Sometimes by official fiat on the highest levels, as when in 2000 Pope St. John Paul II declared St. Thomas More the patron saint of statesmen and politicians. More often than not, however, saintly patronages are the result of folk piety, hallowed by time and sanctioned by custom. Some have even come about as a result of comical error: St. Agatha, who is featured in Christian art with her severed breasts on a tray, is a patron saint of bakers because illiterate peasants thought that the two objects she was holding were loaves of bread.

Because of this sometime slaphappy development, there is no definitive or tidy list of patron saints; indeed, one often finds several different saints being invoked as patrons for the same cause, or one saint for several different causes. The dynamic dimension of this practice has even inspired us to make a few suggestions of our own. Most of these, we admit, are ridiculous and without an iota of magisterial backing, but if they actually work and a saint answers your prayers, we take all the credit. We figure that no harm can come from recommending prayer to a member of the canonized communion of saints, if it is offered in the right spirit. We also hope that the saint will forgive us for the unsolicited recommendation—indeed, we're counting on the fact that he or she kind of has to forgive us.

HOW TO USE THIS BOOK

1. FOLLOW THE SAINTS ON THE CALENDAR

There are several ways to profit from *Drinking with Your Patron Saints*. You can start by following the saint to create an occasion. Find out when the feast day of a particular saint is and host a celebration in his or her honor. Our alphabetical list of the saints includes the dates both in the traditional 1962 calendar and in the 1969 and 2002 versions from after Vatican II.

If you are a policeman, you will want to keep St. Michael's Day (September 29) or St. Jude's (October 28);

if you are a fireman, you will want to observe St. Florian's (May 4). Keeping the feast day of the patron saint of your occupation is an ancient and praiseworthy tradition. In the Middle Ages, different guilds would have great celebrations on their patron's feast, and some occupations still do. French milliners, for example, continue to celebrate the feast of St. Catherine of Alexandria with hat-making contests held on November 25. Be sure to invite your coworkers no matter what their religious affiliation: it will be an occasion for wet evangelization. Our chapter on causes will help you to determine which potential saints' days to keep an eye on for the future.

NAME DAYS

And then there is your name. The feast day of the saint after whom you were named is called your "name day." If your first name is Phil, your name day is the feast of St. Philip the Apostle (May 11) or St. Philip Neri (May 26); if your name is Dorothy, it is St. Dorothea's Day (February 6). And if your name is Mary, well, you've got it made with a wide array of feasts honoring the Mother of God from which to choose.

Some Catholic cultures around the world still celebrate name days with as much gusto as birthdays. A charming book from the 1960s called *My Nameday: Come for Dessert* includes dessert recipes for kiddie parties in honor of your child's patron saint. Consider *Drinking with Your Patron Saints* the grown-up version of that. I can add, on a personal note, that my family and I have grown to love the celebration of name days. While the birthday remains the occasion for worldly festivity and gratitude to God for the gift of life, the name day affords a chance to consider our divine adoption into eternal life through our baptism and to draw closer to the heavenly sponsor whose name we bear.

But what, you may ask, should I do if my first name isn't explicitly Christian? Over the years, parents' name choices have grown less devotional and more colorful—literally in some cases, as with Amber, Auburn, and Cyan. (And what's the deal with naming your kids after jobs that no longer exist, like Cooper and Tanner? I await the day when I meet someone named Solo Saxophonist or Travel Agent.) But this is not an insurmountable problem: use your confirmation name if you have one, or simply attach yourself to a saint with whom you feel a special kinship.

And many names have a Christian origin despite appearances to the contrary. Devotion to the Blessed Virgin Mary, for instance, is hidden under many common girls' names. "Regina," or queen, is for the Queen of Heaven, "Grace" for Our Lady of Grace, "Dolores" for Our Lady of Seven Sorrows, "Soledad" for Our Lady of Solitude, and "Hope" for Our Lady of Hope or Our Lady of Perpetual Help. Similarly, your name may simply be a variation of a saint's name. If you are Caitlyn, Karen, or Kathleen, you share a name with Saints Catherine of Alexandria and Catherine of Siena. Do a little research into the history and meaning of your name, and you may be surprised by its connection to a saint.

2. INVITE THE SAINTS, OR SACRALIZE THE SECULAR CALENDAR

So far we have been talking about planning a celebration around the feast day of a saint, but you can just as easily "invite the saint" to other occasions by incorporating his or her memory into just about any event or gathering. Are a group of coworkers going out for a drink after hours? Order drinks in honor of the patron saint of your shared profession. Are you going on a fishing or hunting trip with friends? Don't forget to invite Saints Peter and Andrew, patrons of fishermen, or Saint Hubert, patron of hunters, to the evening libation.

Is there some news event you wish to celebrate? When astronomers announce the discovery of a new star or meteor, fill the glass in honor of St. Albert, patron of scientists.

What about a personal milestone? If you have just published an article or book, toast to the patron saint of authors, St. Francis de Sales. If you bought a new house, break it in with a celebration honoring St. Joseph. And if your child is going off to college, make sure the going-away party includes drinks for St. Thomas Aquinas, patron of universities and students.

Whatever the event, do not hesitate to infuse the secular with the sacred, to introduce some festive piety and a grateful memory of the communion of saints into an otherwise worldly or mundane occasion. Remember: as a Jesuit casuist will be the first to tell you, although it is not okay to drink while you pray, it is okay to pray while you drink.

TAKE A SICK DAY

As for patron saints of maladies, how about a celebration when the illness has ended? Celebrate your friend's first anniversary of being cancer-free with drinks honoring St. Peregrine. Rejoice over the thyroid medication your spouse is now on with a cocktail for St. Cadoc, patron of glandular problems. Is your new antidepressant working like a charm? Give payment to the pharmaceutical company that made it, but give thanks to God and St. Raphael, patron saint of druggists. And don't be afraid to bend the limits of irony or the canons of good taste. How about a St. Fiacre's Feast against hemorrhoids? Remember, the Church sanctions the use of black humor, which is why St. Lawrence, who famously declared upon being slowly roasted alive on a grill, "You can turn me over; I am done on this side," became the patron saint of comedians and cooks.

However you use this book, may your patron saints inspire you and intercede for you, bringing you good health and godly prosperity.

Part One
Patronages from the Sublime to the Ridiculous

Our own suggestions, which are to be taken with a grain of salt and a shot of tequila, appear in italics.

ABANDONED CHILDREN Ivo, who even as a layman cared for the poor and orphaned

ABORTION Mary, Our Lady of Guadalupe, probably because her famous image on Juan Diego's tilma shows her to be with Child

ABDOMINAL PAINS Elmo, who was disemboweled

ABUSE VICTIMS Monica, who lived with an abusive husband

ACCOUNTANTS Matthew, who was a tax collector

ACTORS Vitus, because of his patronage of dancers

ADOLESCENTS (See Youth)

ADOPTED CHILDREN Thomas More, who took in two orphans, one as his adopted child and the other as his ward

ADVERTISING AND ADVERTISERS Bernardine, who had a knack for messaging with few words and powerful images

ADVOCATES Ivo, who was a lawyer before becoming a priest

AIDS PATIENTS Peregrine, probably because he was a patron of another incurable disease, cancer

Thérèse of Lisieux, probably because she was a patron of another incurable disease, tuberculosis

AIRCREWS Mary, Our Lady of Loreto, whose home flew from Nazareth to Italy

AIR TRAVELERS Mary, Our Lady of Loreto, whose home flew from Nazareth to Italy

Joseph of Cupertino, who levitated while celebrating Mass

AIRPLANE PILOTS Joseph of Cupertino (See above)

Thérèse of Lisieux, who was loved by pilots of the French Air Force in World War I

ALCOHOLISM Monica, who had a minor drinking problem as a girl

ALPS INHABITANTS AND TRAVELERS Bernard of Montjoux, who cared for Alpine pilgrims

ALZHEIMER'S *Albert, who suffered memory loss two years before his death*

AMALFI (ITALY) Andrew, whose relics are there

AMBULANCE DRIVERS Michael, who transports souls from this life to the next

AMERICAN CATHOLIC SOLDIERS Mary, Our Lady of the Immaculate Conception, because she is also the patron of the United States

THE AMERICAS Mary, Our Lady of Guadalupe, so decreed by the pope

AMPUTEES Anthony, who miraculously reattached a foot

ANESTHETISTS AND ANESTHESIOLOGISTS René Goupil, a medical professional who endured tremendous pain under torture

ANGLERS (See Fishermen)

ANIMAL WELFARE SOCIETIES Francis of Assisi, who was kind to animals

ANIMAL ATTACKS Vitus, who was untouched by a lion set upon him

ANIMALS Blaise, since animals came to him on their own for assistance

Francis of Assisi, who was kind to animals

Nicholas of Tolentino, who healed sick animals

APOLOGISTS Catherine of Alexandria, who refuted fifty anti-Christian philosophers

Thomas Aquinas, who brilliantly explained the faith

APPENDICITIS Elmo, who was disemboweled

APPRENTICES Don Bosco, who had an apostolate for the youth

ARCHDIOCESE OF SANTA FE Francis of Assisi, after whom Santa Fe is named

ARCHDIOCESE OF DUBUQE (IOWA) John Mary Vianney, who was a friend of the archdiocese's founding bishop—after the bishop hit him!

ARCHDIOCESE OF PHILADELPHIA Peter and Paul, perhaps because their staunch defense of the faith was needed to counteract nineteenth-century anti-Catholic prejudice

ARCHDIOCESE OF SAN FRANCISCO Francis of Assisi, after whom San Francisco is named

ARCHDIOCESE OF WASHINGTON, D.C. Matthew, who was a reviled tax collector!

ARCHEOLOGISTS Helen, who dug up the True Cross

ARCHERS Hubert, who is the patron saint of hunters
Sebastian, who was martyred *the first time* by archers

ARCHITECTS Barbara, who installed windows in honor of the Trinity
Thomas the Apostle, because he tried to build a king a dwelling place in Heaven

ARCHIVISTS Lawrence, who guarded the Church's written documents

ARMENIA Jude, who evangelized there

ARMORERS George, because he is portrayed in armor
Barbara, who is associated with explosives

ARMORIES Lawrence, possibly because he was martyred on a gridiron

ARMS DEALERS Adrian, who is featured in art with swords and knives

ARROW SMITHS Sebastian, who was martyred *the first time* by archers

ARTHRITIS Alphonsus Liguori, who had a severe case of it

ARTILLERYMEN Barbara, who is a patron saint of explosives

ARTISTS Luke, who allegedly painted images of Our Lady

ASIA MINOR John the Evangelist, who evangelized there

ASTRONAUTS Joseph of Cupertino, who levitated during Mass (look Ma: no gravity!)

Asylums (and the mentally ill) Dymphna, whose insane father murdered her after she refused to marry him

Athletes Sebastian, who was a tough saint and patron of soldiers

Attorneys Catherine of Alexandria, who refuted fifty philosophers in a court-like debate

Thomas More, who was once London's most successful lawyer

Austria Florian, who was popular in German-speaking countries

Joseph, so decreed in 1675

Authors Francis de Sales, who was a successful Catholic author

John the Evangelist, whose books in the New Testament render him a patron of writing

Automobile drivers (See Motorists)

Aviation (See Flying)

Babies Brigid, who was allowed to mystically nurse the infant Jesus

Bakers Agatha, whose severed breasts in Christian art were mistaken for loaves

Honoratus, because of a baking miracle involving his nursemaid

Lawrence, who was grilled alive

Bankers Cajetan, who founded a bank

Matthew, who was a tax collector

Michael, who was appointed patron of bankers because they needed extra protection

Nicholas, because of his association with pawnshops and money bags

BAPTISM John the Baptist, for obvious reasons

BARBERS Louis IX, who is a patron of high culture

BARBITURATES Barbara, after whom barbiturates are named

BARGAIN HUNTERS AND BLACK FRIDAY *Francis de Sales (get it?)*

BATTLE Michael, who successfully battled Lucifer

BEARS (FOR OR AGAINST) *Gall, who rebuked a bear that later became his faithful companion*

Magnus, to whom a bear showed the location of valuable iron ore

BEGGARS Giles, who was crippled like a beggar

BELGIUM Joseph, so decreed in 1679

BELL FOUNDERS Agatha, possibly because she is invoked against volcanic eruptions, which bells warned of

BICYCLE RIDERS (See Cyclists)

BIKERS (See Motorcyclists)

BIRD DEALERS John the Baptist, who is portrayed with a dove (the Holy Spirit) above his head

BIRDS Gall, probably because his name means "rooster"

BLACKSMITHS Brigid, who is associated with farm work

Eligius, who was a skilled metalworker

Leonard, who is linked to iron chains (no pun intended)

BLINDNESS Raphael, who cured Tobias of blindness

BLOOD DONORS Mary, Our Lady of the Thorns, so decreed in 1981 because of a devotion in Parma, Italy

Boaters and boat owners Adjutor, who miraculously saved boatmen from a whirlpool

Bohemia Joseph, so decreed in 1665

Bolivia Mary, Our Lady of Copacabana, who was crowned queen of that country in 1925

Bomb technicians Barbara, who is a patron of explosives because her father was practically pulverized by a lightning bolt

Bookkeepers Matthew, who was a tax collector

Booksellers Thomas Aquinas, who is associated with book learning

Bootblacks Nicholas, who is a patron saint of children

Boulevardiers *Philip Neri, who liked to cruise the streets of Rome*

Boy Scouts George, who was a model of chivalry

Brain tumors Catherine of Alexandria, who became a patron saint of head ailments after being beheaded

Brass workers and founders Barbara, possibly because her patronage of explosives extended to other dangerous jobs

Breast cancer Agatha, whose breasts were severed during torture and miraculously restored
Giles, who received milk from a deer

Breastfeeding Giles, who received milk from a deer

Brewers Augustine, whose Augustinian order made much beer in the Middle Ages
Dorothy, who was burned alive in a manner similar to malt-drying

Lawrence, who was grilled alive in a manner similar to malt-drying

Nicholas, whose patronage of inns extends to the most popular item on the menu

Thomas the Apostle, whose (traditional) feast on December 21 was the last day for brewing beer in Norway

Wenceslaus, who allegedly passed a law protecting local brewers

BRIDEGROOMS Louis IX, who was a great husband and father

Nicholas, whose patronage of brides extended to grooms

BRIDES Dorothy, who was mocked for being a bride of Christ

Nicholas, who helped three poor maidens get married

BRIDGE BUILDERS AND BRIDGES Bénézet, who built a beautiful bridge in France

Peter, who as Supreme "Pontiff" is a "bridge builder" between man and God

BRIGANDS Leonard, who is held accountable for the ex-cons he freed from prison

BROOM MAKERS Anne, who is a patron saint of all things domestic

BUILDERS Barbara, who commissioned three windows to be built

Louis IX, who is a patron of high culture

Mary, Our Lady of Loreto, whose home flew from Nazareth to Italy

Thomas the Apostle, who is a patron of architects

Burns John the Evangelist, who miraculously survived a scalding in oil

Businessmen Homobonus, who was a successful businessman

Butchers Adrian, who is portrayed with knives

George, who is portrayed with a sword or lance

Lawrence, probably because of his ties to cooking

Luke, probably because he is already patron of the related profession of surgeon (gulp!)

Peter, who heard an angel say about some animals, "Arise, kill, and eat"

Button makers Louis IX, who is a patron of high culture

Cab drivers (See Taxi drivers)

Cabinetmakers Joseph, who was a carpenter

Canada Joseph, to whom Canada was consecrated in 1624

Lawrence, on whose feast day the St. Lawrence River was discovered

René Goupil, who was the first North American martyr

Cancer Peregrine, who was miraculously cured of cancer

Cannoneers Barbara, who is a patron of explosives

Canon lawyers Ivo, who was one

Captives Joan of Arc, who was one (thanks to the English)

Carpenters Joseph, who was one

Carters Catherine of Alexandria, who is associated with wheels

Carvers Blaise, who was tortured with steel wool combs

CATERPILLARS Magnus, who protected crops from vermin

CATHOLIC ACTION Paul, who evangelized the Gentiles

CATHOLIC PRESS Francis de Sales, who was a successful Catholic author

CATHOLIC SCHOOLS Thomas Aquinas, who was a model Catholic scholar and teacher

CATS Gertrude, who was already being invoked against mice

CATTLE Brigid, who is associated with farm work

Roch, whose protection against contagious disease extends to cattle

Sebastian, whose protection against contagious disease extends to cattle (at least in Spain)

CEMETERY KEEPERS Joseph of Arimathea, who buried Jesus' body

CENTRAL AFRICA Thérèse of Lisieux, who is a patron saint of foreign missions

CHAMPIONS Drausinus, who "guarantees" victory if you stay all night in his chapel

CHANDLERS Honoratus, because of a baking miracle involving his nursemaid

CHARITY Mary, Our Lady of Charity, who is a model of charity

CHEMICAL ENGINEERS Barbara, who is a patron of explosives and precision

CHICAGO POLICE DEPARTMENT Jude, who was so appointed when devotion to him spread in Chicago

CHICKEN FARMERS Brigid, who was one

Childbirth Anne, the mother of the Blessed Virgin Mary and patroness of all things domestic

Elmo, who is the patron saint of abdominal pains

Leonard, whose prayers helped a queen give birth safely

Childless people Anne, who was childless before having the Blessed Virgin Mary

Anthony, perhaps because he is portrayed with the infant Jesus

Gummarus, who was one

(See also Women who wish to become mothers)

Children Nicholas, who according to legend resurrected three butchered children

Children learning to speak or walk Zeno, who was a renowned teacher of children

Children's nurses Foillan (it's unclear why)

Chimney sweeps Florian, who is a patron of fire safety

Chivalry George, who saved a maiden from a dragon

Choirinophobia Mark, whose relics were hidden in a crate of pork so that Muslim inspectors would not touch them

Cholera Roch, who helped people with contagious diseases

Chefs Lawrence, who was roasted alive

Chronic illness Lidwina, who was bedridden for thirty-eight years after an ice-skating accident

Church (See Universal Church)

Cinderella situations Zita, a handmaid who was treated badly by her masters

CIVIL DEFENSE VOLUNTEERS Padre Pio, because they asked the pope for Pio's patronage and got it

CIVIL SERVANTS Matthew, whose patronage of accountants and customs officers extends to civil servants
Thomas More, who was one

CIVILIAN WAR VICTIMS Mary, Our Lady Queen of Peace, who was so appointed by Pope John XXIII

CLOCKMAKERS Peter, possibly because of the "tears of St. Peter" legend

CLOTHWORKERS Homobonus, whose patronage of merchants extends to clothworkers

COIN COLLECTORS Eligius, who was the king's master of the mint

COLLEGES Thomas Aquinas, who was a university professor

COMEDIANS Lawrence, who cracked a joke while being roasted alive
Vitus, because of his patronage of dancers

COMMUNISM Joseph, who was made patron of the Church's "vast campaign…against world Communism" in 1937

COMPOSITORS John the Evangelist, whose books in the New Testament render him a patron of fields related to printing

COMPUTERS, COMPUTER PROGRAMMERS AND SCIENTISTS Isidore, whose patronage of the internet extends to computers and those who work on them

CONDEMNED CRIMINALS Dismas, who was one

CONFECTIONERS Joseph, who is a patron of many different workers

Honoratus, because of a baking miracle involving his
 nursemaid

 Lawrence, who is a patron saint of chefs

CONFESSION Giles, who is (inaccurately) portrayed as
 Charlemagne's confessor

CONFESSORS Alphonsus Liguori, who was an excellent
 moral theologian

 Padre Pio, who could read hearts and was a great confessor

CONSTRUCTION WORKERS (See Builders)

CONTAGIOUS DISEASES Roch, who helped people who had
 them

 Sebastian, who posthumously stopped a plague in Rome

CONVERTS Augustine, who was one

COOKS Lawrence, who was roasted alive

COPPERSMITHS Leonard, who is associated with metals
 because freed prisoners sent him their chains

COSTERMONGERS Fiacre, who tended a garden and distributed herbs

COUGARS (OF THE HUMAN VARIETY) *Anne, who according
 to one legend was married three times*

COUGHS Blaise, who is the patron saint of throat ailments

COURT CLERKS Thomas More, who was a lawyer and
 judge

COURTIERS Gummarus, who was one

COWBOYS *Sebastian of Aparicio, who was the world's first
 charro*

COWHERDS Gummarus, who was kind to his field hands

CRAFTSMEN Eligius, who was a skilled metalworker

CREDIT CARDS *Expeditus, who is a patron of money problems and against procrastination (perfect, right?)*

CRIPPLES Giles, who was crippled from a hunting accident

CROATIA Joseph, so decreed by the Croatian Parliament in 1687

CROPS Magnus, who protected a crop from vermin (Also see Harvests)

CRUSADERS Louis IX, who was one

CUBA Mary, Our Lady of Charity: Cuba has a beloved statue of her from the sixteenth century

CURSILLO MOVEMENT Paul, who was a powerful evangelizer

CUSTOMS OFFICERS Matthew, whose patronage of tax collectors and accountants extends to customs officers

CUTLERS Lucy, whose throat was slit by a knife

CYCLISTS Mary, Our Lady of Ghisallo, whose roadside shrine in Italy is a popular cycling destination

CZECH REPUBLIC Wenceslaus, who was a duke of Bohemia

DAIRY WORKERS Brigid, who was one

DANCERS Vitus, who was seen in prison with angels dancing around him

DANGERS AT SEA Elmo, who is loved by sailors for being unafraid of lightning

Michael, because of an ancient devotion at the famous Mont Saint-Michel on the coast of Normandy

THE DEAD Michael, who transports souls from this life to the next

THE DEAF Cadoc, who healed the deaf

Francis de Sales, who learned sign language to teach a deaf man the faith

DEATH OF CHILDREN Frances of Rome, who lost two children to the Plague

Louis IX, two of whose eleven children died in infancy

DEER *Giles, who received milk from a deer*

DEGREE CANDIDATES Joseph of Cupertino, who struggled on exams

DEMENTIA *Albert, who suffered memory loss two years before his death*

DEMOCRATIC REPUBLIC OF THE CONGO Mary, Our Lady of the Immaculate Conception, because of the Marian devotion of Belgian missionaries to that country

DENTISTRY Apollonia, whose teeth were pulled out

Foillan (it's unsure why)

DESPERATE CASES Jude: because his name resembles Judas Iscariot's, people turned to him only when they were desperate

DIABOLICAL OBSESSION Raphael, who saved Sara from a demon harassing her

DIABOLICAL POSSESSION Dymphna, patroness of the mentally ill, who is invoked against diabolical possession in the event that a patient's madness is not psychological but demonic

Michael, who cast Lucifer out of Heaven

DIFFICULT MARRIAGES Gummarus, who had one

Louis IX, who had a very good marriage to Queen Margaret

Monica, who had one

DIRTY DANCING *John Mary Vianney, who forbade it*

DISAPPOINTING CHILDREN Monica, who was disappointed in her son Augustine before he converted

DISCOTHEQUES *Mary, Our Lady of Copacabana (get it?)*

DISTILLERS Louis IX, possibly because he is a patron of high culture

DOCTORS (See Physicians)

DOG ATTACKS Vitus, who was untouched by a lion set upon him

DOGS Hubert, whose patronage of hunters extends to their dogs

Roch, who was helped by a dog that licked his wound and brought him food

DOMESTIC ANIMALS George, who killed a sheep-eating dragon

DOUBTERS Joseph, who suffered doubt after seeing that his espoused, the Blessed Virgin Mary, was with child

Thomas the Apostle, who doubted Jesus' resurrection before being vividly corrected

DRAFT DODGERS *John Mary Vianney, who, though conscripted, failed to serve in Napoleon's army*

DROWNING Adjutor, who miraculously saved boatmen from a whirlpool

DRUGGISTS (See Pharmacists)

THE DYING Joseph, who died in the arms of Jesus and Mary

Nicholas of Tolentino, who comforted the dying and freed souls from Purgatory

Dysentery Lucy, whose patronage of hemorrhaging extends to dysentery

Ecologists Francis of Assisi, who was on good terms with God's creatures

Economists *Bernardine, who was one of the first theologians to write a complete book on economics*

Editors Don Bosco, who published popular religious books

Francis de Sales, who was a successful Catholic author

Egypt Mark, who evangelized there

El Salvador Mary, Our Lady Queen of Peace, a statue of whom inexplicably appeared in the city of San Salvador carried by a donkey. The statue was solemnly crowned in 1921

The elderly Anthony, whose patronage of the poor and oppressed extends to the elderly

Mary, Our Lady of Consolation, so decreed in 1961

Embroiderers Clare, who made ornate vestments

Louis IX, who is a patron of high culture

EMTs Michael, who transports souls from this life to the next

Enemies of religion Sebastian, who was unafraid of Christianity's enemies

Enemy plots Drausinus, who is the patron of invincibility

Engaged couples Joseph, who was a model of purity and trust during his engagement and marriage to the Blessed Virgin Mary

Valentine, who is a patron saint of lovers

ENGINEERS Joseph, whose patronage of carpenters extends to engineers

Patrick, who oversaw construction of churches and taught the Irish to build arches with lime mortar instead of dry masonry

ENGLAND George, to whom England has been devoted for a very long time and whose cross is on the English flag

Michael, to whom the English had an early devotion

ENGRAVERS John the Evangelist, whose books in the New Testament render him a patron of fields related to printing

ENTREPRENEURS Bernardine, who helped a manufacturer of playing cards diversify

ENTRYWAYS Isidore (get it?)

THE ENVIRONMENT Francis of Assisi, who was on good terms with God's creatures

EPILEPSY Dymphna, whose patronage of mental illness extends to nervous disorders

Vitus, who is associated with nervous disorders because he is associated with that strange twitching calling dancing

EQUATORIAL GUINEA Mary, Our Lady of the Immaculate Conception, so decreed in 1986

EQUESTRIANS Anne, whose patronage of the home extended to the barn, the creatures therein, and those who rode them

ESSENTIAL OILS Nicholas, whose relics emit a healing oil

Ethiopia George, to whom Ethiopians have been devoted for a very long time

Excluded people Patrick (it's unclear why, but the infamous "No Irish Need Apply" signs come to mind)

Expedited shipping *Expeditus, a patron of speedy cases*

Eye problems Clare, who had them

Lucy, whose eyes were gouged out and miraculously restored

Raphael, who cured Tobias of blindness

Fainting Valentine, whose patronage of lovers extends to swooners

Faith in the Blessed Sacrament Anthony, who inspired a mule to kneel in adoration before the Eucharist

Families Joseph, whose headship of the Holy Family extends to all families

Famine victims Cadoc, who filled his parents' cellar with food when he was still in the womb

Farmers George, who is portrayed on horseback and who killed a sheep-eating dragon

Farmers' markets *Fiacre, who gave herbs from his garden to pilgrims*

Farriers (See Blacksmiths)

Fathers Joseph, who was an excellent foster father of Our Lord

Fear of night Giles, who lived alone in a dark cave

Fear of snakes Patrick, who drove the snakes from Ireland

FEMALE SERVANTS Zita, who was one

FENCING Michael, who is portrayed with a sword

FERRYMEN AND THEIR PASSENGERS Christopher, who was a ferryman

FEVER Barbara, who is invoked against sudden death

FINAL PERSEVERANCE Alphonsus Liguori, who persevered in his faith despite a long and bitter trial at the end of his life

FINANCIAL OFFICERS Matthew, whose patronage of tax collectors and accountants extends to financial officers

***FINDING A PARKING SPOT WHEN YOU ARE RUNNING REALLY LATE** Jude, who is the patron saint of desperate cases*

FIRE Agatha, whose patronage against volcanoes extends to fire

Nicholas of Tolentino, who miraculously extinguished fires

FIREFIGHTERS Florian, who was one

FIREWORKS MANUFACTURERS Barbara, who is a patron of explosives

FISHERMEN Andrew, who was one

Nicholas, whose patronage of seafarers extends to fishermen

Peter, who was one

Zeno, a bishop who liked to fish in order to provide for himself

FISHMONGERS Andrew, who was a commercial fisherman

Peter, who was a commercial fisherman

FISTULAS Fiacre, who is the patron saint of hemorrhoids

Floods Florian, who was drowned

Florence (Italy) Philip Benizi, who was born in the Florentine district of Oltrarno

Florists Dorothy, who miraculously gave someone flowers

Fiacre, who kept a very good garden

Thérèse of Lisieux, who promised to send roses from Heaven

Flour merchants Honoratus, because of a baking miracle involving his nursemaid

Flower growers Thérèse of Lisieux, who promised to send roses from Heaven

Flying Joseph of Cupertino, who levitated during Mass

Thérèse of Lisieux, who was loved by the French Air Force in WWI

Foot problems Peter, whose foot was injured shortly before his martyrdom

Foreign missions Thérèse of Lisieux, who prayed tirelessly for the missions

Foresters Gummarus, who miraculously restored a tree

Forests Giles, who lived in one as a hermit

Fortifications Barbara, perhaps because she is often portrayed alongside the tower in which her father locked her up

Fractures Gummarus, who miraculously restored a tree

France Joan of Arc, who led the French army against the English

Louis IX, who is France's only canonized king

Mary, Our Lady of the Assumption, so decreed in 1922
because of French Marian devotion

Michael, because of Mont Saint-Michel in northern
France

Thérèse of Lisieux, who was French

FREIGHT SHIPS AND THEIR CREWS Christopher, who was
a ferryman

FRENCH AIRCREWS Mary, Our Lady of the Assumption,
who is depicted "flying" to Heaven

FRENCH CANADA Anne, who as a member of the extended
Holy Family was much loved in colonial French Canada

FRENZY Peter, probably because he betrayed Christ in a
panic

FRIENDSHIPS John the Evangelist, the "beloved disciple"
who wrote on the subject and was a close friend of Our
Lord

FUGITIVES Brigid (it's unclear why)

FUNERAL EMPLOYEES Dismas, who joined Jesus in Paradise when he died

Joseph of Arimathea, who buried Jesus' body

GAMBLING Bernardine, who preached against it successfully

GAMERS AND GAMBLERS Cajetan, who helped gamblers
down on their luck

GARAGE AND GAS STATION WORKERS Eligius, who was a
skilled fixer

GARDENERS Adam, who kept the first one

Christopher, whose staff miraculously bloomed

Dorothy, who miraculously gave flowers to someone

Fiacre, who kept a very good garden

Gertrude: fine weather on her feast day is an auspicious time to plant a garden

GARMENT WORKERS Homobonus, whose patronage of merchants extends to clothworkers

GENTILE CHRISTIANS Paul, who evangelized them

GEOMETERS Thomas the Apostle, whose patronage of architects extends to geometers

GEORGIA (THE EURASIAN COUNTRY) George, after whom the country is named (in English)

GERMANY Michael, to whom Germans have had a devotion since the Middle Ages

GILDERS AND GOLDSMITHS Clare, who made ornate gilded vestments

GLAMORGAN (WALES) Cadoc, who lived there

GLANDULAR DISORDERS Cadoc (for reasons that are unclear)

GLAZIERS Lucy, whose name means "light" and whose patronage extends to jobs involving light

GLOVE MAKERS Gummarus (it's unclear why)

GOLDSMITHS Eligius, who was a skilled goldsmith

GOOD FORTUNE Cajetan, who is a patron of gamblers

GOOD WEATHER Clare, whose name means "clear"

GOUT Andrew, perhaps because of his patronage of Scotland!

GRANDMOTHERS Anne, who is the grandmother of Jesus Christ

GRASSHOPPERS Magnus, who saved a crop from vermin

GRAVEDIGGERS Joseph of Arimathea, who buried Jesus's body

GREECE Andrew, who is said to be the founder of the Church in Constantinople

Nicholas, because of his popularity there

Paul, who preached there

GREEN BERETS (U.S. ARMY SPECIAL FORCES) Philip Neri: the Green Berets named him their patron because he "embodied the traits of the ideal Special Forces Soldier: Selfless, Superb Teacher, and Inspirational Leader"

GREETING CARD MANUFACTURERS Valentine, because of his patronage of lovers

GREETINGS Valentine, because of his patronage of lovers

GROCERS Michael, possibly because grocers are in danger of being attacked by robbers

GUARDIAN ANGELS Raphael, the angel who guarded Tobias and Sara

GUNNERS Barbara, who is a patron of explosives

HABERDASHERS Louis IX, who is a patron of high culture

Michael (for reasons that are unclear)

HAIL Magnus, who protected a crop from devastation

HAIRDRESSERS Louis IX, who is a patron of high culture

THE HANDICAPPED (MENTALLY) Joseph of Cupertino, who probably had a mental handicap

THE HANDICAPPED (PHYSICALLY) Giles, who was lame

A HAPPY DEATH Joseph, who died in the arms of Jesus and Mary

HAPPY MEETINGS Raphael, who arranged the meeting of Tobias and Sara

HARVESTERS Peter, possibly because of the Gospel verse "The harvest is great but the laborers are few"

HARVESTS Anthony, who miraculously restored a damaged crop

Florian, who is invoked against damaging water (rain, floods, and so forth)

HATMAKERS Michael (it's unclear why)

(Also see Haberdashers and Milliners)

HAWAII Mary, Our Lady Queen of Peace, the patroness of the Sacred Heart Fathers, who evangelized there

HEADACHES Catherine, who was beheaded

HEALERS Brigid, who was one

HEART PATIENTS Philip Neri, who had a miraculously enlarged heart and violent palpitations

HEMORRHAGES Lucy, whose prayers saved her hemorrhaging mother

HEMORRHOIDS Fiacre, whose name resembles the French word for a small tumor

HERMITS Giles, who was one

HERNIAS Gummarus, who is invoked against fractures and ruptures of all kinds

HESITATION Joseph, who hesitated when he discovered that the Blessed Virgin Mary was with Child

HIGHWAYS John the Baptist, who made straight the way of the Lord (no joke)

HOARSENESS Bernardine, who struggled with it

HOLISTIC MANAGEMENT METHODS OF ANIMAL HUSBANDRY
  Magnus, who used a dragon to rid the area of vermin

A HOLY DEATH Andrew Avellino, who had one
  Joseph, who died in the arms of Jesus and Mary

HOMEMAKERS Anne, who is a patron saint of all things
  domestic
  Monica, who was a model homemaker despite being
    married to a lout

HOPELESS CAUSES Jude: because his name resembles
  Judas Iscariot's, people turned to him only when they
  were desperate

HORSEMEN Anne, whose patronage of the home extended
  to the barn and the creatures therein
  George, who killed a dragon while on horseback

HORSES Eligius, who posthumously cured a horse

HORSE WHISPERERS *Zeno, who calmed down a horse by
  making the sign of the cross over it*

HORTICULTURALISTS Adam, who kept the very first garden
  Fiacre, who kept a very good garden

HOSPITALS, HOSPITAL WORKERS, AND PATIENTS Jude,
  whose patronage of hopeless causes extends to those
  who sometimes feel hopeless in hospitals and those
  who care for them

HOUSE HUNTERS AND SELLERS Joseph, who has been a
  patron saint of real estate since the sixteenth century
  thanks to some nuns

HUMOR Philip Neri, who was zany and hilarious

HUNTERS Hubert, who had a vision of the cross while hunting

IMPENITENCE Barbara, whose father died impenitent

INCEST Dymphna, whose insane father wanted to marry her

INDIA Thomas the Apostle, who evangelized there

INFERTILITY Giles, perhaps because he is a patron of breastfeeding

INFORMATION TECHNOLOGY (IT) Isidore, whose patronage of the internet extends to IT

INNER MONGOLIA Mary, Our Lady of the Immaculate Conception, so decreed in 1914

INNKEEPERS Nicholas, who converted a murderous innkeeper

INSECT BITES Mark, whose patronage of skin problems extends to insect bites

THE INTERIOR LIFE Joseph, who lived privately with Jesus and Mary and was a master of the interior life

THE INTERNET Isidore, who compiled the world's first database

INTESTINAL DISORDERS Elmo, who was disemboweled

INVALIDS Roch, who had a bad thigh wound

INVINCIBILITY Drausinus, who "guarantees" victory if you stay all night in his chapel

IRELAND Brigid, a longtime patron of the Emerald Isle
Patrick, Apostle of Ireland

ITALY Francis of Assisi, who was Italian

JAMAICA Mary, Our Lady of the Assumption, so decreed in 1951

JANUARY BLUES Padre Pio, who was so appointed by an office of the bishops of England

JEWELERS Eligius, who was a skilled goldsmith

JIMMY LEG (RESTLESS LEG SYNDROME) *St. Vitus, who was seen in prison with angels dancing around him and thus gave his name to St. Vitus' Dance, the uncontrollable jerking caused by the disease now known as Sydenham's chorea*

JOB SEEKERS Cajetan, who helped people down on their luck

JOINERS Joseph, who was a carpenter
Thomas the Apostle, who was a carpenter

JORDAN John the Baptist, who did his baptizing in the Jordan River

JOURNALISTS Francis de Sales, who was a successful Catholic author

JOY Philip Neri, who is called the Apostle of Joy

JUDGES Ivo, who was one before becoming a priest

JURORS Catherine, whose patronage of attorneys extends to jurors

JUSTICE Martin de Porres, who endured racial injustice

JUVENILE DELINQUENTS Don Bosco, who had an apostolate for the youth

KIDNEY DISEASE Valentine (it's unclear why)

KILCHOMAN (SCOTLAND) Comman, after whom Kilchoman is named

Kings Louis IX, who is France's only canonized king

Knee problems Roch, who had a bad wound in his thigh (which is close enough)

Knife grinders Catherine of Alexandria, who is associated with wheel-shaped devices

Knights Hospitaller John the Baptist: the hospital after whom the Knights were named was named after Saint John

Knuckle sandwiches *Nicholas, who reputedly smacked the heretic Arius*

Lace makers Louis IX, who is a patron of high culture
Anne, who is a patron saint of all things domestic

The laity Frances of Rome, who was an active laywoman

Lambs John the Baptist, who called Jesus the Lamb of God

The lame Giles, who was crippled

Lamp makers Mary, Our Lady of Loreto (for unclear reasons)

Laundry workers Clare, who made ornate vestments

Lawyers Ivo, who was one before becoming a priest
Mark, who concisely recorded Christ's life
Thomas More, who was one

Lay apostolates Paul, who brought in new laity to the Church

Lead workers Sebastian, possibly because he is also a patron of arrow smiths

Lepers George, whose protection of the helpless extends to lepers

Giles, who is a patron of the outcast

LIBRARIANS AND LIBRARIES Catherine of Alexandria, whose patronage of law and education extends to libraries

Lawrence, who guarded the Church's written documents

Mark, possibly because he faithfully preserved St. Peter's memories of Jesus Christ in his Gospel

LIGHTNING Magnus, who protected a crop from lightning

Vitus, who survived a bad lightning storm

LIONS Mark, whose symbol is a lion

LITHOGRAPHERS John the Evangelist, whose books in the New Testament render him a patron of fields related to printing

LLANCARFAN (WALES) Cadoc, who lived there

LOCKSMITHS Peter, one of whose symbols is a pair of keys

LONGEVITY Peter, who lived a relatively long life

LONGSHOREMEN Nicholas, whose patronage of seafarers extends to longshoremen

THE LOSS OF A PARENT Louise de Marillac, who lost her mother and father by the age of fifteen

LOST ARTICLES Anthony, whose prayers made even the Devil demand that a thief return Anthony's stolen Bible

LOST KEYS Zita, who was given the keys of her master's household

LOVERS Raphael, who arranged a happy marriage for Tobias and Sara

Valentine, whose feast falls the day before a Roman courtship festival

LUMBERJACKS Gummarus, who is a patron of foresters

LUMBERSEXUALS *John the Baptist, who looks like one (especially if you substitute a flannel shirt for the camel hair)*

MACHINISTS Hubert, whose patronage of metalworkers extends to machinists

MAGICIANS Don Bosco, who used magic tricks to get young people interested in religion

MAIDS Zita, who was one

MAIL Anthony, perhaps because he is also a patron saint of travelers

MALTA Paul, who was shipwrecked there

MARBLE WORKERS Louis IX, who is a patron of high culture

MARCHING AUXILIARIES Vitus, because of his patronage of dancers

MARITIME PILOTS Nicholas, who saved some sailors off the coast of Lycia

MARRIED COUPLES Joseph, who had a very successful marriage with the Blessed Virgin Mary

MASSIVE SCREWUPS *Adam, who kicked himself and the entire human race out of Paradise*

MATHEMATICIANS Barbara, who became a patron of the precise

Hubert, whose patronage of metalworkers extends to people who need to be precise

MECHANICS Catherine of Alexandria, who is patron of wheels and the machines attached thereto

MEDAL COLLECTORS Eligius, who was the king's master of the mint

MEDICAL PROFESSIONS Luke, who was a physician

MEDICAL TECHNICIANS Albert, whose patronage of scientists extends to medical technicians

MEDIOCRE EQUESTRIANS *Francis de Sales, who fell from his horse three times in one day*

MEMORY LOSS *Albert, who suffered memory loss two years before his death*

THE MENTALLY ILL Dymphna, whose insane father murdered her when she refused to marry him

Fillan, who had a "miraculous" sanitizing pool named after him

Gertrude, whose garden was associated with healing

Raphael, whose patronage of health extends to mental health

MERCHANTS Francis of Assisi, who used to be one

Homobonus, who was a successful merchant

Nicholas, whose patronage of pawnshops extends to merchants

METALWORKERS Eligius, who was one

Hubert, whose "keys" (a charm against rabies) are made of metal

#METOO *Dymphna, whose insane father sexually assaulted and murdered her*

METROSEXUALS *Francis of Assisi, who cured himself of vanity by changing clothes with a beggar*

MEXICAN YOUTH Don Bosco, who was so declared because

of his work with youth

MEXICO Joseph, so decreed in 1555

Mary, Our Lady of Guadalupe, because of her apparition in that country

MEZCAL *Mary, Our Lady of Guadalupe: the tilma bearing her image is made from the same plant as mezcal*

MICE AND RATS Gertrude, who is portrayed with mice as symbols of souls

MIDWIVES Dorothy, who was mocked for being a bride of Christ

MIGRAINES Catherine of Alexandria, whose patronage of headaches extends to migraines

MILITARY ENGINEERS Barbara, who is a patron saint of explosives

MILKMAIDS Brigid, who was one

MILLERS Catherine of Alexandria, who is a patron of wheel-like devices

Honoratus, because of a baking miracle involving his nursemaid

MILLINERS Catherine of Alexandria, who is patron of those who use wheel-like devices

MINERS Anne, who is the genetrix of "silver" (Mary) and "gold" (Jesus)

Barbara, who is a patron saint of those who use explosives

Lawrence, possibly because he was martyred on a gridiron

MISSIONARIES Thérèse of Lisieux, who prayed for missionaries

MISSIONS TO THE CHINESE Joseph, so decreed in 1678 because the Lazarist missionaries had a devotion to him

MISSIONS Paul, who evangelized the Gentiles

MONEY ISSUES Expeditus, who is a patron saint of speedy cases

MONEY MANAGERS Matthew, whose patronage of tax collectors and accountants extends to money managers

MORAL THEOLOGIANS Alphonsus Liguori, who was one

MOTHERS Anne, who is the mother of the Blessed Virgin Mary

Monica, who was a good mother despite having a difficult son like St. Augustine

MOTORCYCLISTS Mary, Our Lady of Castellazzo, whose shrine is inundated on her feast day by motorcyclists seeking a blessing

MOTORISTS Christopher, a ferryman who is a patron saint of travelers

Frances of Rome, who used her wagon extensively to help the poor

Sebastian of Aparicio, who built a road and introduced native Americans to the use of wheeled vehicles

MOUNTAINEERS AND MOUNTAIN CLIMBERS Bernard, who helped travelers through the Alps

MUSICAL INSTRUMENTS Cecilia, who sang in her heart to the Lord alone when she heard profane music at her wedding

MUSICIANS Cecilia, who sang in her heart to the Lord alone when she heard profane music at her wedding

NATURAL SCIENTISTS Albert, who was a great naturalist

NAVAL OFFICERS Francis of Paola, who miraculously sailed across the Strait of Messina to Sicily on his cloak

NAVIGATORS Elmo, who is loved by sailors for being unafraid of lightning

Francis of Paola, who miraculously sailed across the Strait of Messina to Sicily on his cloak

NEARSIGHTEDNESS, AND TURNING IT TO YOUR ADVANTAGE *Alphonsus Liguori, who took off his glasses at the theater so he wouldn't see bad things*

NEEDLEWORKERS Louis IX, who is a patron of high culture

Clare, who made ornate vestments

NEIGHBORHOOD WATCH Sebastian, who is a patron saint of policemen

NERVOUS DISORDERS Dymphna, whose patronage of mental illness extends to nervous disorders

Vitus, after whom St. Vitus' Dance is named

NET MAKERS Peter, who was a commercial fisherman

NEW CALEDONIA Mary, Our Lady of the Assumption, so decreed in 1963

NEW DISCOVERIES Helen, who found the True Cross

NEWBORN BABIES Zeno, who was a renowned teacher of children

NEWLYWEDS Dorothy, who was mocked for being a bride of Christ

Nicholas, who helped three poor maidens get married

NIGERIA Patrick, because of the Irish missionaries who evangelized that country

NIGHTMARES Raphael, who saved Sara from diabolical obsession

NOTARIES Luke, for his accuracy as an Evangelist

Catherine of Alexandria, whose patronage of lawyers extends to notaries

Ivo, whose patronage of lawyers extends to notaries

Mark, for his accuracy as an Evangelist

NUNS Brigid, who started women's religious life in Ireland

NURSES FOR THE MENTALLY ILL Dymphna, who founded a hospital and whose insane father murdered her when she refused to marry him

NURSES Catherine of Alexandria, whose patronage of purity extends to children and their nurses

Raphael, who is a healing angel and patron saint of healers

OIL MERCHANTS Nicholas, whose relics emit a fragrant and healing oil

OIL REFINERS Honoratus, because of a baking miracle involving his nursemaid

OLD-AGE PENSIONERS Mary, Our Lady of Consolation, so decreed in 1961

OLD-CLOTHES DEALERS Anne, perhaps because she is a patron saint of the home, whence come old clothes

OPEN SORES Peregrine, who had one on his leg

OPHTHALMOLOGISTS Lucy, whose eyes were gouged out and miraculously restored

THE OPPOSITION OF CHURCH AUTHORITIES Joan of Arc, who was unjustly condemned by an English Church tribunal

THE OPPRESSED Anthony, who was a champion of the poor

OPTICIANS Hubert, whose patronage of metalworkers extends to those who need to be precise

Lucy, whose eyes were gouged out and miraculously restored

ORATORS Augustine, who was a great orator

Catherine of Alexandria, who publicly defeated fifty philosophers in a debate

ORDER OF TEUTONIC KNIGHTS George, who was a model of chivalry

ORDER OF THE GARTER George, who was a model of chivalry

ORDNANCEMEN Barbara, who is a patron saint of explosives

ORPHANS Ivo, who even as a layman cared for the poor and orphaned

THE OUTCAST Giles, who became a patron of the crippled and hence of the outcast

OVERSLEEPING Vitus, who was an early riser

PAINTERS Luke, who allegedly painted an icon of the Blessed Virgin Mary

PAKISTAN Thomas the Apostle, who evangelized there

PALESTINIAN CHRISTIANS George, who was one

PALLBEARERS Joseph of Arimathea, who buried Jesus' body

PAPERMAKERS John the Evangelist, whose books in the New Testament render him a patron of fields related to writing

PAPUA NEW GUINEA Michael, so decreed in 1979

PARAGUAY Mary, Our Lady of the Assumption, so decreed in 1951

PARAMEDICS Michael, who transports souls from this life to the next

PARATROOPERS Michael, who defeated Lucifer in an aerial battle

PARENTS OF LARGE FAMILIES Louis IX, who had eleven children

PASTRY CHEFS Honoratus, because of a baking miracle involving his nursemaid

PAWNBROKERS Nicholas, who is associated with the three money bags he used to help three poor maidens get married

PEASANTS Lucy (it's unclear why)

***PEDESTRIANS** Philip Neri, who liked to cruise the streets of Rome on foot*

PENCIL MAKERS Augustine, whose patronage of theologians extends to writing instruments and their makers

PEOPLE ASSOCIATED WITH THE SEA Francis of Paola, who miraculously sailed across the Strait of Messina to Sicily on his cloak

PEOPLE IN TEMPORAL DISTRESS Joseph, who, as head of the Holy Family, understood temporal distress

PEOPLE OF MIXED RACE Martin de Porres, who was half Spanish and half African

PEOPLE REJECTED BY RELIGIOUS ORDERS Louise de Marillac, who was rejected by the Capuchins

People ridiculed for their piety Zita, who was mocked for her goodness by her masters and her fellow servants

People with an older brother who acts like he's God's representative on earth *Andrew, the younger brother of St. Peter*

People working in windowless cubicles *Albinus, whose name means "white"*

Perfumers Nicholas, whose relics emit a fragrant oil

The persecuted Joseph, who was persecuted by Herod

Peru Joseph, so decreed in 1957

Pest control *Philip Neri, who told a lady who had an aversion to roaches in a hospital to take the first one she saw and put it in her mouth. When she went to the hospital to do so, all the roaches had miraculously vanished. She returned to the saint, who smiled knowingly*

Pharmacists Raphael, who made a paste to heal Tobias of blindness

The Philippines Mary, Our Lady of Guadalupe, because the Philippines were once under the jurisdiction of Spanish Mexico

Mary, Our Lady of the Immaculate Conception, so decreed in 1578

Philosophers Catherine of Alexandria, who converted fifty of them to the faith

Thomas Aquinas, who had a mastery of philosophy

Physicians Luke, who was one

Raphael, who is a healing angel and patron of healers

Roch, who helped people with contagious diseases

Sebastian, who was healed after facing a firing squad of archers

PIETRELCINA (ITALY) Padre Pio, who was from there

PILGRIMS Christopher, who is a patron of travelers

PINCUSHIONS *Sebastian, who looked like one after facing a firing squad of archers*

PIONEERS Joseph, who traveled into the unknown when fleeing Herod

PIOUS PROFITEERS *Bernardine, who helped a manufacturer print holy cards*

PIRATE ATTACKS Albinus, who ransomed people kidnapped by pirates

THE PLAGUE Roch, who helped people with the plague

Sebastian, who posthumously stopped a plague in Rome

POISON John the Evangelist, who nullified poison in his drink by blessing it

POLAND Florian, whose patronage of German-speaking countries migrated to Poland

POLICE Jude, who was named a patron saint of the Chicago Police Department

Michael, who is a protector of the innocent

Sebastian, who was captain of the Praetorian Guard

POLITICIANS Thomas More, who was chancellor of England

POOR PEOPLE Anthony, on whose feast day "St. Anthony's bread" is given to the poor

Giles, who is a patron of the outcast

Joseph, who was relatively poor
Lawrence, who as deacon served the poor
Nicholas, who helped three poor maidens get married
POPES Michael, whose patronage of the Universal
Church extends to the pope in particular
Peter, who was the first pope
PORTERS Leonard, perhaps because of his association
with prisons
PORTUGAL Anthony, who was born in Lisbon
POTTERS Catherine of Alexandria, who is a patron of
wheel-like devices
PRACTICAL JOKES *Philip Neri, who played a lot of them,
mostly on himself*
PREACHERS Catherine of Alexandria, who publicly
refuted fifty philosophers
PRECISION INSTRUMENT MAKERS Hubert, whose patronage
of metalworkers extends to those who need to be precise
PRIESTS (ESPECIALLY DIOCESAN) John Mary Vianney,
who was an exemplary parish priest
PRINTERS Augustine, because of his association with
writing
PRINTING PRESSES Brigid, perhaps because she estab-
lished a school of art that made illuminated manu-
scripts
PRISON GUARDS Adrian, who was a Palatine guard in the
Roman Empire
PRISONERS OF WAR Leonard, whose heavenly intercession
freed one

PRISONERS Barbara, who was imprisoned by her father
Joan of Arc, who was imprisoned by the English
Leonard, who freed prisoners
Louis IX, who was imprisoned during a Crusade
Nicholas, who was imprisoned for slapping the heretic
Arius
Roch, who died in prison

PROCRASTINATION Expeditus, who did not delay in converting

PROLONGED SUFFERING Lidwina, who suffered for decades

PROSPECTORS *Magnus, who found iron ore thanks to a bear*

PUBLIC EDUCATION (PERU) Martin de Porres, because the bishops of Peru requested his patronage and got it

PUBLIC HEALTH SERVICES (CHIEFLY IN PERU) Martin de Porres, because the bishops of Peru requested his patronage and got it

PUBLISHERS Don Bosco, who published highly popular religious books

PUERTO RICO John the Baptist, whom the explorer Juan Ponce de Leon chose to be the patron of the island

PURITY Catherine of Alexandria, whose name means "pure" and who was
Joseph, who had a chaste marriage with the Blessed Virgin Mary

RABIES Hubert, whose patronage of hunters extends to their dogs and the danger of rabies

RACIAL HARMONY Martin de Porres, a saint of mixed race

who humbly endured prejudice

RADIOLOGISTS Michael, whose patronage of the sick extends to those who administer dangerous radium treatments

RADIOTHERAPISTS Michael, whose patronage of the sick extends to those who administer dangerous radium treatments

RANCHERS George, who is portrayed on horseback and who killed a sheep-eating dragon

REFUGEES Joseph, who was one when he fled to Egypt

RELIEF FROM PESTILENCE Roch, who helped people with contagious diseases

REPENTANT MURDERERS Nicholas, who converted a murderous innkeeper

RESTAURATEURS Lawrence, who is a patron saint of chefs
Nicholas, whose patronage of inns extends to restaurants

RHEUMATISM Alphonsus Liguori, who had severe arthritis

ROAD BUILDERS Sebastian of Aparicio, who built a road more than four hundred miles long

ROASTERS Lawrence, who was roasted alive

ROBBERS Leonard, who is held accountable for the ex-cons he freed from prison

ROMANIA Andrew, who preached as far as Kiev (Ukraine)

RUSSIA Andrew, who preached as far as Kiev (Ukraine)
Nicholas, who is immensely popular with the Eastern Orthodox
Joseph, so decreed in 1930 in responses to the outrages committed against the Church by the Soviets

Thérèse of Lisieux, who prayed for foreign missions such as those that would come to be in the Soviet Union

SADDLERS George, who is a patron of horses and things pertaining to them

Lucy, whose name means "light" and whose patronage extends to jobs requiring light late into the night

SAFE JOURNEYS Nicholas, whose patronage of seafarers extends to all travelers

SAILORS Christopher, who was a ferryman

Elmo, who is loved by sailors for being unafraid of lightning

Francis of Paola, who miraculously sailed across the Strait of Messina to Sicily on his cloak

Michael, because of an ancient devotion at the famous Mont Saint-Michel on the coast of Normandy

Nicholas, who saved some sailors off the coast of Lycia

Peter, who was one (as a commercial fisherman)

SALESMEN Lucy (it's not clear why)

SALTPETER WORKERS Barbara, who is the patron saint of miners

SCAVENGER HUNTS *Joan of Arc, who miraculously found a buried sword*

SCHOLARS Catherine of Alexandria, who prevailed in a debate with fifty philosophers

Thomas Aquinas, who was an exemplary scholar

SCHOOLCHILDREN Don Bosco, who had an apostolate for the youth

SCHOOLS Thomas Aquinas, who was a great university professor

SCIENTISTS Albert, who was a fine naturalist

SCOTLAND Andrew, because Scotland had some of his relics until they were destroyed during the Scottish Reformation (the archbishop of Amalfi and Pope Paul VI have since given additional relics of the saint to the Catholic cathedral in Edinburgh)

SCRIBES Catherine of Alexandria, whose patronage of law and education extends to scribes

SCROFULOUS DISEASES Mark, who was flayed alive

SCRUPULOSITY Alphonsus Liguori, who suffered from terrible scruples at the end of his life

SCULPTORS Louis IX, who was a patron of high culture

SEASICKNESS Elmo, who is loved by sailors for being unafraid of lightning

SEAMSTRESSES Anne, who is a patron saint of all things domestic

Catherine of Alexandria, who is associated with wheel-like devices

Lucy, who is a patron saint of all jobs requiring light (her name means "light")

SECOND HELPINGS *Thomas More (get it?)*

SECURITY FORCES Michael, because of his protection of Heaven

SECURITY GUARDS Matthew, whose patronage of tax collectors and accountants extends to security guards

SENIOR CITIZENS (See Elderly)

SEPARATED SPOUSES Gummarus, who separated from his difficult wife

SHEPHERDS John the Baptist (See Lambs)

SHIP BUILDERS Peter, who was a boat owner

SHIPWRECKS Anthony, who is a patron saint of travelers

   Catherine of Alexandria, who had a reputation as a
      powerful intercessor

SHIPWRIGHTS Peter, who was a boat owner

SHOEMAKERS Homobonus, whose patronage of merchants
      extends to cobblers

   Peter, whose shoes every pope tries to fill

*SIBLING RIVALRY Comman, whose brother Cumine the
      White was more distinguished*

THE SICK Louise de Marillac, whose Daughters of Charity
      were exemplary in their care for the sick

   Michael, who has patronized the sick since ancient
      times

SILVERSMITHS Eligius, who was a skilled metalworker

SINGERS Cecilia, who sang in her heart to the Lord alone
      when she heard profane music at her wedding

SKATERS Lidwina, who had a bad ice-skating accident

SKIERS Christopher, who ferried across a river

   Lidwina, who had a bad accident while enjoying ice-
      skating, another winter sport

   Mary, Our Lady of Graces, because of an Italian devo-
      tion in the ski town of Folgaria

SLEEPWALKING Dymphna, whose patronage of diabolical
      possession extends to sleepwalkers out of a medieval
      fear that there was something demonic going on with
      somnambulism

Smelters Barbara, who is the patron saint of miners

Hubert, whose "keys" (a charm against rabies) are made of metal

Snake attacks Vitus, who was untouched by a lion set upon him and is thus invoked against other kinds of animal attacks

Snakes Magnus, who saved a crop from vermin

Patrick, who drove the snakes out of Ireland

Soap boilers Florian, possibly because of his association with fire and water

Social media Expeditus, who is invoked against wasting time

Social workers Joseph, because of his care for the Holy Family

Louise de Marillac, whose Daughters of Charity were exemplary in their care for the needy

Software developers Isidore, whose patronage of the internet extends to IT

Soldiers Adrian, who was one

George, who was one

Joan of Arc, who was one (albeit a noncombatant)

Sebastian, who was one

Solomon Islands Michael, so decreed in 1979

Souls in Purgatory Gertrude, whose patronage of pilgrims extends to the next life

Nicholas of Tolentino, whose prayers freed souls detained there

South Africa Mary, Our Lady of the Assumption, so decreed in 1952

SOUTH KOREA Mary, Our Lady of the Immaculate Conception, so decreed in the mid-nineteenth century and reiterated by the pope in 1984

SOUTHERN BAPTISTS *John Mary Vianney, who preached against drinking and dancing*

SPAIN Mary, Our Lady of the Immaculate Conception, so decreed in 1962

SPANISH CATTLE BREEDERS Mark, because they asked the pope for his patronage and got it

SPAS John the Baptist, who is tied to healing waters
John the Evangelist, who emerged from a cauldron of boiling oil looking better than when he went in

SPEEDY CASES Expeditus, who did not delay in converting to Christianity

SPEEDY FOOD DELIVERY *Philip Benizi, who prayed to the Blessed Mother when his monks ran out of food. No sooner had he finished than there was a knock at the door. The monks opened the door and found ten big baskets of bread.*

SPINSTERS (See Unmarried women)

SPUR MAKERS Giles, who is a patron of blacksmiths

SRI LANKA Lawrence: Because his namesake Lawrence de Almeida was leader of the Portuguese colonists, a chapel to the saint was dedicated in present-day Colombo, Sri Lanka

STAINED GLASS MAKERS Lawrence, because of his association with furnaces
Lucy, whose name means "light" and whose patronage extends to jobs requiring light

Starvation Anthony, who miraculously restored a damaged crop

Statesmen Thomas More, who was a great statesman and student of political philosophy

Stepparents Thomas More, who was one

Stockbrokers Matthew, whose patronage of tax collectors and accountants extends to stockbrokers

Stonemasons John the Baptist, who made straight the way of the Lord

Louis IX, who was a patron of high culture

Thomas the Apostle, who is a patron saint of builders

Storms Vitus, who survived a bad storm that killed many pagans

Stress relief Padre Pio, who was so appointed by an office of the bishops of England

Strokes Andrew Avellino, who had one as he was about to celebrate Mass

Struma (the skin disease) Mark, who was flayed alive

Students Albert, who was an excellent teacher

Joseph of Cupertino, who struggled as a student

Thomas Aquinas, who was an excellent teacher

Students (especially female) Catherine of Alexandria, who was a wise young woman

Students who are struggling *John Mary Vianney, who struggled with his seminary studies*

Sudden death Andrew Avellino, who suffered a stroke when beginning to celebrate Mass but lived long enough to receive the viaticum

Barbara, whose father died suddenly after executing her

Catherine of Alexandria, whose would-be killers died suddenly when they tried to kill her on a spiked wheel

SURFERS Christopher, whose patronage of ferrymen extends to surfers

Patrick, who miraculously helped a leper surf on an altar stone

SURGEONS Foillan, perhaps because he is portrayed kneeling with a spear in his side

Luke, who was a physician

Roch, who helped people with contagious diseases

SURVEYORS Thomas the Apostle, who is a patron saint of architects and builders

SURVIVALISTS Giles, who lived alone in the woods

SWIMMERS Adjutor, who miraculously saved boatmen from a whirlpool

SYPHILIS George, whose patronage of soldiers extends to diseases brought on by their vices

SYRIA Barbara, who lived there

TAILORS Catherine of Alexandria, who is patron of wheel-like devices

Homobonus, whose patronage of merchants extends to tailors

John the Baptist, who made his own clothes

TANNERS Lawrence, who was roasted alive

TANZANIA Mary, Our Lady of the Immaculate Conception, so decreed in 1984

TAPESTRY WORKERS Francis of Assisi, who used to be a cloth merchant

Taverns *John Mary Vianney, whose preaching shut down four of them in his town*

Tax collectors Matthew, who was one

Taxi drivers Fiacre: a Parisian hotel named after him became the first taxi stand

Christopher, who was a ferryman

Teetotalers *John the Baptist, who was one*

Television actors, writers, and so forth Clare, who saw a Mass projected on her room wall

Television Clare, who saw a Mass projected on her room wall

Tequila *Mary, Our Lady of Guadalupe: the tilma bearing her image is made from the same plant as tequila*

Test takers Joseph of Cupertino, who struggled taking exams

Textile workers Andrew (it's unclear why)

Theft Dismas, who was a repentant thief

Theologians Augustine, who was an excellent theologian

Catherine of Alexandria, who refuted fifty philosophers with her theology

Paul, who is in a sense the first Catholic theologian

Thomas Aquinas, who was an excellent theologian

Thieves Dismas, who was crucified for being a thief

Leonard, who is held accountable for the ex-cons he freed from prison

Nicholas, who appeared to two juvenile delinquents and showed them the error of their ways

Throat ailments Blaise, who saved a boy from choking

Lucy, whose throat was slit

THYROID PROBLEMS Cadoc (it's unclear why)

TILE MAKERS Roch (it's unclear why)

A TOOTHACHE OF A PERSON *Apollonia, the patron of tooth-aches*

TOOTHACHES Apollonia, whose teeth were pulled out under torture

TOY MAKERS Nicholas, whose patronage of children extends to toy makers

TRADE PROTECTIONISTS *Wenceslaus, who protected the local beer industry with draconian laws*

TRADESMEN Homobonus, who was a successful business-man

Joseph, who was a carpenter

TRANSPORTATION INDUSTRY (IN MEXICO) Sebastian of Aparicio, who built a four-hundred-mile-long road and taught native Americans how to use wheeled vehicles

TRAPPERS Hubert, whose patronage of hunters extends to trappers

TRAVEL HOSTESSES Anthony, who traveled extensively

TRAVELERS Anthony, who traveled extensively

Christopher, a ferryman who transported the Christ Child

Gertrude, who was already a patron of pilgrims

Joseph, who guarded the Holy Family during their journey to Egypt and back to Nazareth

Nicholas, who journeyed to the Holy Land

Raphael, who guided Tobias and Sara on their journey

TROOPS OF SAINT GEORGE George, who was an early model of chivalry

TRUSS MAKERS Foillan (it's unclear why)

TUBERCULOSIS Thérèse of Lisieux, who died of it

TUNNELLERS Barbara, who is a patron saint of those who use explosives

TURKEY John the Evangelist, who evangelized there

TURNERS (LATHE OPERATORS) Anne, who is a patron saint of all things domestic

TYPESETTERS John the Evangelist, whose books in the New Testament render him a patron of fields related to printing

__UBER DRIVERS__ Christopher, who is already a patron of motorists

Fiacre, who is already a patron of cab drivers

UKRAINE Andrew, who preached as far as Kiev

UNBORN CHILDREN Joseph, who protected the Virgin Mary as she bore the Infant Jesus on their way to Bethlehem

Mary, Our Lady of Guadalupe

UNDERTAKERS (See Funeral employees)

UNEMPLOYED PEOPLE Cajetan, who helped people down on their luck

UNITED STATES OF AMERICA Mary, Our Lady of the Immaculate Conception, because the American bishops requested her patronage from the pope and got it in 1847

U.S. MARINE CORPS George, who was a great warrior

U.S. AIR FORCE Michael, who defeated Lucifer in an aerial battle

Thérèse of Lisieux, who started by patronizing the French Air Force and then upgraded

U.S. ARMED FORCES Michael, who is a warrior par excellence

U.S. ARMY CAVALRY George, who was a cavalryman

U.S. ARMY FIELD ARTILLERY Barbara, who is a patron saint of those who use explosives

UNIVERSAL CHURCH Joseph, who as head of the Holy Family extends his patronage to the Church

  Michael, who guards the Church as he once guarded Israel

  Peter, the Rock upon whom Christ built the Church

UNIVERSITIES Thomas Aquinas, who was an excellent university professor

UNMARRIED WOMEN Andrew, whose feast coincides with folk games for divining one's future husband

  Anne, who according to legend was good at finding a husband—three of them, to be precise

  Catherine of Alexandria, whose patronage of purity extends to maidens

  Nicholas, who helped three poor maidens get married

UPHOLSTERERS Mary, Our Lady of the Immaculate Conception (it's unclear why)

URGENT CAUSES Expeditus, who did not delay in converting to Christianity

VEGETARIANS STUCK AT A DINNER MEANT FOR CARNIVORES *Nicholas of Tolentino, a vegetarian who blessed a chicken dinner; the roasted chicken miraculously flew away*

VENEREAL DISEASES (STDs) Fiacre, whose herbs treated a variety of maladies

VERMIN Magnus, who miraculously saved a crop from vermin

VERMONT Mary, Our Lady of Graces, who is the patroness of skiers

VETERINARIANS Eligius, who posthumously cured a horse

VIETNAM (SOUTH) Joseph, so decreed in 1952

VINTNERS Lawrence, possibly because as deacon he handled the Precious Blood at Mass

VOCALISTS Cecilia, who sang in her heart to the Lord alone when she heard profane music at her wedding

VOCATIONS Alphonsus Liguori, who fostered them

VOLCANOES Agatha, a native of Sicily who is invoked against Mt. Etna erupting

WAITERS AND WAITRESSES Zita, who was a domestic servant

WAREHOUSES Barbara, whose patronage of explosives extends to places that can hold them

WATER (DANGERS FROM) Florian, who was drowned

WATER SKIERS *Patrick, who miraculously helped a leper cruise on an altar stone behind a ship*

WEAVERS Blaise, who was tortured with steel wool combs

Catherine of Alexandria, who is a patron of wheel-like devices

WET NURSES Agatha, whose patronage of breasts extends to wet nurses

WHEELWRIGHTS Catherine of Alexandria, who is a patron of wheels

WIDOWS Frances of Rome, who became one after a forty-year marriage

Louise de Marillac, who used her widowhood to found a religious order

WINDSURFING *Francis of Paola, who miraculously wind-surfed using his cloak*

WIVES Monica, who was a model wife despite being married to a lout

WOMEN IN LABOR (See Childbirth)

WOMEN WHO WISH TO BECOME MOTHERS Andrew (it's unclear why)

WOMEN WHO WISH TO FIND A GOOD HUSBAND Anne, who according to legend was good at finding a husband—three of them, to be precise

WOODCUTTERS Gummarus, who is a patron of foresters

WOOL COMBERS Blaise, who was tortured with steel wool combs

WOOL SPINNERS Catherine of Alexandria, who is a patron of wheel-like devices

WORKERS Cajetan, who helped people trying to make a living

Joseph, who was one

WRITERS Francis de Sales, who was a successful Catholic author

Lucy, whose name means "light" and whose patronage extends to jobs requiring light

YACHTSMEN Adjutor, who miraculously saved boatmen from a whirlpool

YOUTH Don Bosco, who had an apostolate for the youth

Padre Pio, who was good with the youth despite being banned from teaching them by his enemies

Raphael, who guided the young Tobias and Sara

ZAIRE Mary, Our Lady of the Immaculate Conception (it's unclear why)

ZOOS AND ZOO KEEPERS   Francis of Assisi, because of his love of animals

PART TWO
PATRON SAINTS FROM ADAM TO ZITA

I f two dates are listed after the saint's name, the first is according to the traditional 1962 calendar and the second (in parentheses) according to the new, post–Vatican II calendar. If there is only one date, it is observed by both calendars or the traditional calendar only.

And if you can't find a saint, consult *Drinking with the Saints* (Regnery, 2015) or *Drinking with Saint Nick* (Regnery, 2018).

ADAM, DECEMBER 24 (BYZANTINE CALENDAR)

It may sound strange to think of our first parents as holy figures, but according to tradition both Adam and Eve felt really, really bad about the whole Fall of Man business and spent the rest of their years—or rather centuries—doing penance. The Byzantine calendar observes the feast of Adam and Eve on December 24, and while the Western Church has never formally recognized Adam as a saint, the unofficial commemoration of his feast day with mystery plays about the Temptation in the Garden included representations of the Tree of the Knowledge of Good and Evil and the Tree of Life, which ultimately led to our modern Christmas tree. And, of course, as the only gardener of Paradise, Adam is the natural choice for patron of gardeners and horticulturalists.

ADAM'S APPLE

1 oz. apple brandy or applejack   ½ oz. dry vermouth
½ oz. gin   dash of green Chartreuse

Put ice in a mixing glass and add ingredients, starting with the Chartreuse. Stir well and strain into a chilled cocktail glass.

PATRONAGES | Gardeners and horticulturalists
Suggested Patronage Massive screwups

LAST CALL

Throw a garden party with all your friends who share your joy of getting your hands dirty and make the following toast: "Through the intercession of the old Adam, may the new Adam, our Lord Jesus Christ, grant us success in our gardens and even greater success in the cultivation of our souls."

After the second round, find a way to work in a devilishly clever quote from Dorothy Parker: "You can lead a horticulture, but you can't make her think."

St. Adjutor, April 30

St. Adjutor, or Ayoutre, (d. 1131) was a noble Norman who fought with distinction in the Crusades for sixteen years before being captured and imprisoned in Jerusalem. He was miraculously freed by St. Mary Magdalen and St. Bernard of Tiron and returned home to become a monk. Adjutor is invoked against drowning because one day he heard of a whirlpool in the River Seine that was claiming the lives of many boatmen. Rushing to the scene, he made the sign of the cross over the whirlpool and sprinkled it with holy water, making it instantly disappear.

There is an old cocktail called a Sink or Swim, but it failed to impress our panel of taste testers, and so we turned to Balcones Distilling mixologist Andrew Anderson for help. He did not disappoint.

Sink or Swim #2

by Andrew Anderson

1½ oz. Balcones Texas "1"
   single malt whisky
¾ oz. lemon juice

½ oz. orgeat syrup
1 cherry

Pour liquid ingredients into a shaker filled with ice and shake forty times. Strain into a chilled cocktail glass and garnish with cherry. We leave it to you whether you want the cherry to sink or swim.

PATRONAGES | Boaters, drowning, swimmers, yachtsmen

St. Adrian of Nicomedia, September 8

St. Adrian (d. 306) was head of the elite Imperial Palatine guards known as the Herculiani but, after witnessing the courage of Christians being tortured, gave it all up and converted. Because Adrian was stretched to death over an anvil, he is represented in art armed with a sword next to an anvil and thus became the patron saint of arms dealers, soldiers, and butchers. In fact, in northern Europe during the Middle Ages, Adrian was second only to St. George as a military saint.

To celebrate St. Adrian, take a shot at anything evocative of firearms. You can steal from St. Barbara and have an Artillery cocktail or from St. Joan of Arc and have a French 75. Or try a Gunfire, a classic British military mixed drink that is traditionally served on Christmas Day to soldiers in their beds by their officers, when on deployment.

Gunfire

1 cup of hot black tea (Austra-   1½ oz. rum
  lian version: substitute coffee)

Pour the rum into the tea or coffee and stir.

The offerings of two craft breweries, Bare Arms Brewing in Waco, Texas, and Call to Arms in Denver, Colorado, would also be appropriate choices.

PATRONAGES | Arms dealers, butchers, prison
guards, soldiers

LAST CALL

Pray to Adrian for a good deal the next time you attend a
gun show. Then go home, fix yourself a libation, and make the
following toast: "May St. Adrian, patron saint of the Second
Amendment, arm us with heavenly virtues."

ST. AGATHA, FEBRUARY 5

A beautiful native of Sicily, Agatha (d. ca. 251) consecrated her life to God and refused to apostatize, even when a lustful governor had her breasts cut off (hence her depiction in Christian art holding a tray with two breasts on it). Happily, she was miraculously cured that night by a mysterious visitor to her cell who identified himself as an apostle of Christ.

Agatha died from other wounds inflicted by her tormentors and quickly became a powerful intercessor in Heaven. She is the patron saint not only of, for obvious reasons, breast cancer patients, wet nurses, and torture victims, but also of bakers, all because some folks in the Middle Ages mistakenly thought that her tray was holding loaves of bread. Sicilians turn to her for protection against Mt. Etna, and some contend that she also patronizes bell founders because bells were used to warn the population of volcanoes. But at the risk of sounding Freudian, could the bell makers have made the same mistake as the bakers in interpreting her artistic depiction?

In Sicily, there is a *Denominazione di origine controllata* (DOC) appellation—a seal of approval for regional wines that meet quality standards—of red, white, and rosé named Sant'Agata dei Goto. But if you're in an impish mood, how about a Twin Peaks cocktail? The drink may not have miraculous powers, but you can at least put two of them on a tray to celebrate St. Agatha.

TWIN PEAKS

1½ oz. whisky
½ oz. sweet vermouth

1 tsp. orange liqueur (Cointreau, Grand Marnier, etc.)
1 twist of lemon

Pour all ingredients except lemon twist into a mixing glass with ice and stir forty times. Strain into a cocktail glass and garnish with lemon.

PATRONAGES | Bakers, bell founders, breast cancer, fire, torture victims, volcanoes, wet nurses

LAST CALL

An appropriate toast would be, "To St. Agatha: may we have her faith, her fortitude, and her prayers." An inappropriate toast would be, "To St. Agatha: like the tray she holds, may she always be supportive and uplifting."

ALBERT THE GREAT, NOVEMBER 15

Albertus Magnus (d. 1280) was a Dominican friar, a professor at the Universities of Paris and Cologne, a teacher of St. Thomas Aquinas, and the bishop of Regensburg. Albert had an encyclopedic mind and was a brilliant natural scientist who in some ways anticipated Darwin's work on how species are adapted to their environments. Pius XII understandably made this Doctor of the Church a patron saint of students and natural scientists. But Albert did not have a perfect track record in his academic research. He speculated that *ardea*, the Latin name for heron, came from the fact that its excrement burns (*ardet*) whatever it touches and also claimed that the heron will defend itself from a hawk by aiming its anus at the assailant and shooting excrement at it; if the hawk's wings are hit, they melt.

To honor St. Albert's work on the toxic waste of the hum-flinging heron, we recommend a Mud Pie.

MUD PIE

1½ oz. rye or bourbon
½ oz. orange curaçao
½ tsp. simple syrup

2 dashes Peychaud bitters
1 orange slice, cherry, lemon
   twist

Build (that is, add in the order in which they appear in the recipe) all liquid ingredients in an old-fashioned glass filled with ice. Garnish with orange slice, cherry, and lemon twist.

PATRONAGES | Medical technicians, natural scientists, scientists, students

LAST CALL

Pius XII's statement about Albert can be turned into a toast: "Through the patronage of Albert the Great, may almighty God arouse the hearts and minds of those who devote themselves to the sciences to a peaceful and orderly use of the natural forces, the laws of which, divinely established, they investigate and seek after."

Less sophisticated is the popular toast "Here's mud in your eye," which takes on a whole new meaning in light of Albert's heron. So does the following: "Through the intercession of St. Albert, may the enemies of the Church never know what hit them."

ST. ALBINUS, MARCH 1

St. Albinus, or Aubin, (470–588) was a monk before he reluctantly became the bishop of Angers, France. He was known for his generosity to the poor and for ransoming hostages taken prisoner by pirates on the Loire River.

Drink suggestion: There is a delicious Armagnac made by Château de Saint-Aubin. Stored in limousin oak barrels, this liquor is put on a ship that sails around the world for at least ninety days. Changes in air pressure, humidity, and temperature combine with constant movement to produce a truly exquisite brandy. How fitting that something produced on the high seas should bear the name of the protector against pirates.

The ingredients to the Pirate's Cocktail, however, may be easier to find and cheaper to buy.

Pirate's Cocktail

1¾ oz. dark rum 1 dash Angostura bitters
¾ oz. red vermouth

Pour ingredients into a mixing glass with ice and stir forty times. Strain into a cocktail glass.

PATRONAGE | Against pirate attacks *Suggested Patronage People working in windowless cubicles—because Albinus means "white." (We know: a real knee-slapper. It's funnier after the second round).*

St. Alphonsus Liguori, August 2 (August 1)

St. Alphonsus, born in 1696 in the Kingdom of Naples, enjoyed the music of the theater in his youth but had concerns about some of the risqué costumes and scenes, so he came up with a clever solution. As soon as the curtain rose, the nearsighted saint took off his glasses so he could see nothing on stage. Alphonsus eventually founded the Redemptorist order and became a great moral theologian who stressed the importance of confession. He is invoked against arthritis and rheumatism because he had so severe a case in his old age that he could barely lift his chin (hence the depictions of him stooped over).

Nearly blind by the end of his life, St. Alphonsus was tricked into signing a revised rule of his Congregation that led the pope to remove him as head of the Redemptorists. The Doctor of the Church spent the last seven years of his life as a scorned pariah, and the last three of those years in a terrible "dark night of the soul" involving temptations, scruples, and diabolical illusions. Thanks be to God, Alphonsus held firm and died in peace in 1787. His reputation was vindicated shortly afterwards, with the same pope who had fired him declaring him Venerable.

The Neapolitan cocktail is a sweet way to honor this native of Naples, especially after dinner.

NEAPOLITAN

1½ oz. light rum   ½ oz. Grand Marnier
½ oz. Cointreau

Pour ingredients into a mixing glass with ice and stir until very cold. Strain into a cocktail glass.

PATRONAGES | Arthritis, confessors, final perseverance, moral theologians, rheumatism, scrupulosity, vocations *Suggested Patronages Nearsightedness, and turning it to your advantage*

LAST CALL

After carefully measuring out the drinks for the night, remove your glasses and offer the following toast: "Through the prayers of the good St. Alphonsus, may our Lord grant us the gift of holy perseverance and keep us from all physical and moral rigidity."

ST. ANDREW, NOVEMBER 30

Saint Andrew, one of the twelve apostles and the younger brother of Saint Peter, is the patron of numerous countries and causes, including Russia, Scotland, Greece, and Amalfi, Italy. We have a long section on Andrew in *Drinking with the Saints* (pp. 329–32); here we include two new delicious ways to honor the saint.

R&B Distillers in Edinburgh has a recipe for a St. Andrew's Martini that gives a nod to all of the above. The vodka honors Andrew's patronage of Russia, the Raasay scotch his patronage of Scotland, the Kalamata olive his patronage of Greece, and the Amalfi lemon his patronage of Amalfi (the cathedral of which houses his relics).

A classic White Russian also suits St. Andrew—and The Dude in *The Big Lebowski*.

ST. ANDREW'S MARTINI

1½ oz. Stolichnaya Blue Vodka
¾ oz. dry vermouth
1 Amalfi lemon twist

2 tsps. Raasay While We Wait
   single malt scotch
1 Kalamata olive

Pour all liquid ingredients into a mixing glass with ice and stir forty times. Strain into a cocktail glass and garnish with olive and lemon twist.

WHITE RUSSIAN

2 oz. vodka   1 splash heavy cream
1 oz. Kahlúa liqueur

Pour the vodka and Kahlúa into an old-fashioned glass with ice.
Top with heavy cream and stir.

PATRONAGES | Amalfi (Italy), fishermen and
fishmongers, gout, Greece, Romania, Russia, Scotland, textile
workers, Ukraine, unmarried women, women who wish to
become mothers ***Suggested Patronage*** *Anyone with an older
brother who acts like he is God's representative on earth*

ST. ANDREW AVELLINO, NOVEMBER 10

Even before entering the Theatine order, St. Andrew Avellino (1521–1608) led an exemplary life of chastity. A hand-
some man, he took the tonsure (became a cleric) as a way of
escaping his female admirers. St. Andrew practiced both
canon and civil law until one day a lie slipped from his lips
as he was passionately pleading a friend's case. Cut to the
quick, he left the legal profession.

St. Andrew is the patron saint invoked against strokes
because he died as a result of a stroke that he suffered at the
beginning of a Mass he was celebrating, but not before he
was able to receive the viaticum.

Several miracles are attributed to this humble and loving
servant of God, including the following: "As he was once
returning home late at night from hearing a sick man's confession, a violent storm of wind and rain put out the light that

was being carried before him; but neither he nor his companions were made wet by the pouring rain; and, moreover, a wonderful light shining from his body enabled them to find their way through the darkness."

You too can experience something dark and stormy without getting wet and feel a wonderful light from within when you imbibe a Dark and Stormy.

DARK AND STORMY

2 oz. light rum	ginger beer, chilled
1 oz. lime juice	lime zest
½ oz. simple syrup	lime wheel or slice for garnish

Pour rum, lime juice, and simple syrup into a shaker filled with ice and shake forty times. Strain into a highball glass half-filled with ice. Sprinkle lime zest, and top with ginger beer. Garnish with lime.

PATRONAGES | Apoplexy, diabolical possession, holy death, against strokes and sudden death

LAST CALL
Today, share in St. Andrew's aversion to lying. Raise a glass and say, *In vino veritas*—"In wine, there is truth."

ST. ANNE, JULY 26

Because of a legend that St. Anne was married three times and remained childless until she became the mother of the Blessed Virgin Mary, she is invoked for numerous causes related to marriage, childlessness, and childbirth. Anne's association with eventual domestic bliss also made her a natural ally for everything pertaining to hearth and home, from broom makers and lace makers to seamstresses and "turners" (lathe operators). It is our guess that Anne's protection of the house was extended to the barn, which is why she also patronizes equestrians and stablemen.

But how is Our Lord's grandmother the patroness of miners? By a magnificent twist of medieval folk logic, that's how. Since Our Lord is pure gold and Our Lady pure silver, then is not St. Anne's womb the mine from which these precious metals come?

If the Middle Ages can get away with that line of reasoning, we have one for the Modern Age. Anne's finding herself a man to marry not once but thrice (presumably when she was no spring chicken) earns her the title of All-Time Patroness of Cougars.

To celebrate, mix this semi-original cocktail from *Drinking with the Saints* called the Saint Anne.

SAINT ANNE

1½ oz. light rum   ½ oz. orange curaçao liqueur
¾ oz. lemon juice

Pour ingredients into a shaker filled with ice and shake forty times. Strain into a cocktail glass.

PATRONAGES | Broom makers, childbirth, childless women, equestrians, French Canada, homemakers, horsemen, grandmothers, lace makers, miners, mothers, old-clothes dealers, seamstresses, turners, unmarried women, women who wish to find a good husband

Suggested Patronage Cougars

LAST CALL

Whatever your particular petition to St. Anne, tack on the following ancient folk ditty for all faithful spinsters and cougars:

I beg you, holy mother Anne,
Send them a good and loving man.

ST. ANTHONY OF PADUA, JUNE 13

St. Anthony of Padua (1195–1231) was a native of Portugal and a priest of the Franciscan order who preached with such power that after Pope Gregory IX heard him, the pontiff called him *Arca Testamenti*—a living repository of scripture. St. Anthony is often portrayed with the Infant Jesus because the Divine Child once came to him and showered him with kisses until he responded in kind (perhaps this depiction explains his patronage of childless women). And St. Anthony is the well-known patron saint of lost objects because he raised so many lamentations after his precious copy of the Bible had been stolen that the Devil, exacerbated, told the thief to return it.

Anthony is also the patron saint of faith in the Blessed Sacrament, for good reason. When a man refused to listen to arguments about the Real Presence of Jesus in the Eucharist, Anthony asked him if he would believe if he saw his own mule adore the Blessed Sacrament. The man accepted the challenge but heightened the stakes: he starved his mule for three days and had Anthony and the Eucharist stand opposite a pile of hay. On the day of the test, the hungry mule came in, ignored the hay, approached Anthony, and bent its front legs in adoration before the Eucharist. Upon seeing this, the astonished man knelt down as well. And with alarming polls about Catholics not believing in the Real Presence, we may need more help from Anthony in finding our lost faith than our lost keys.

Like other Franciscans, this Doctor of the Church was a champion of the poor; on his feast day, "St. Anthony's bread" is distributed to the needy. He is a patron of harvests and against starvation because he miraculously restored a crop after it was trampled by a crowd that had come to hear him preach. And we assume that his extensive travels made him a patron of travelers.

But how did Anthony become the patron of amputees? When a young man confessed to Anthony that he had kicked his mother in a moment of anger, the saint absentmindedly said, "That foot deserves to be cut off." The impetuous penitent ran out of the church, grabbed the first axe he could find, and did exactly that. After hearing what had happened, Anthony rushed to the scene and miraculously reattached the severed foot.

The Do Come Round cocktail is a *Drinking with Your Patron Saints* original. Invented by our friends the Wards, it takes its name from an old prayer to St. Anthony:

> Tony, Tony, do come round,
> Something's lost and must be found;
> It's a _____.

DO COME ROUND

by Tom and Katie Ward

1½ oz. bourbon
½ oz. sweet vermouth
1–2 dashes cardamom bitters

½ oz. maraschino liqueur
(Maraska or Luxardo)

Pour ingredients into a mixing glass with ice and stir forty times. Strain into a cocktail glass.

PATRONAGES | Amputees, childless women, the elderly, faith in the Blessed Sacrament, harvests, lost articles, mail, oppressed people, poor people, Portugal, the starving, shipwrecks, travel hostesses, travelers

LAST CALL

A toast: "May St. Anthony help us find our lost articles, make us kind to the poor and oppressed, and increase our faith in the Blessed Sacrament."

ST. APOLLONIA, FEBRUARY 7

Apollonia (d. 249) was an early virgin martyr from Alexandria whose teeth were pulled out in an attempt to make her apostatize. She is frequently depicted in art with her teeth or a pair of pincers and is understandably associated with dentistry and toothaches.

What better way to celebrate St. Apollonia than with a Toothfull cocktail?

TOOTHFULL

by V. A. Tooth

1 dash of Bénédictine liqueur

1½ oz. gin

¾ oz. sweet vermouth

¾ oz. dry vermouth

1 dash of orange bitters

Swill cocktail glass with a dash of Bénédictine. Stir remaining ingredients in a mixing glass with ice until very cold and strain into the cocktail glass.

PATRONAGES | Dentistry and toothaches *Suggested Patronage Against anyone who can be described as a toothache of a person*

LAST CALL

A toast to St. Apollonia: "May she help us get to the Pearly Gates with pearly whites and keep us from the place where there is wailing and gnashing of teeth."

ST. AUGUSTINE OF HIPPO, AUGUST 28

St. Augustine (354–430) is famous for converting to the Catholic faith after a lascivious life. He went on to become bishop of Hippo Regius (in modern-day Algeria), a devastating opponent of the schisms and heresies of his day, and the most influential and important of the Church Fathers—which is saying a lot: there wasn't a dud among them. His autobiography, the *Confessions*, is a spiritual masterpiece and was the second-most-read book in Western Christendom (next to the Holy Bible) before the sixteenth century.

To celebrate St. Augustine, try a *Drinking with the Saints* original that honors his deliverance from the pleasures of the flesh. All the ingredients are inspired by the *Confessions*: honey simple syrup for the "honeyed pages" of the Bible that he read before converting, fig vodka for the fig tree under which he converted, and lemon juice for the bittersweet renunciation of his former lust. The name Lady Continence is based on St. Augustine's vision of the virtue of continence in all its beauty.

Augustine is also a patron saint of brewers. Some think that the saint was given this role because of his dissolute past, but the truth is that although his sins were as scarlet as his books were read, they did not include an abuse of the bottle. Rather, it is because of his spiritual descendants, the Augustinian monks, who were among the best beer makers of the Middle Ages. Today, several breweries carry on this fine tradition. The Van Steenberge brewery is under license from the Augustinian monks of St. Stefanus in Ghent, Belgium, to produce beers which they themselves had been making from 1295 to 1978. In the United States, you will see these beers marketed under the label St. Stefanus instead of Augustijn to avoid legal conflicts with another Augustinian community, the Augustiner brewery in Munich, which also sells beer in America.

LADY CONTINENCE

2 oz. fig vodka
½ oz. lemon juice
simple syrup made from 1½
    tsp. honey and 2½ tsp. water

(warm both in a saucepan
and stir until honey is dissolved)
1 sliced fig for garnish

Pour all ingredients except fig into a shaker filled with ice and shake forty times. Strain into an old-fashioned glass filled with ice and garnish with fig slice.

Note on fig vodka: There is a Figenza fig vodka that is becoming increasingly available in the U.S. But if it has not yet reached your area, you can always make your own. Take 2½ ounces of dried figs cut in half and one vanilla bean and put them in one liter of vodka (we recommend Tito's). Refrigerate for three days, shaking the bottle twice a day. Strain through a cheesecloth.

PATRONAGES | Brewers, converts, orators, pencil makers, printers, theologians

LAST CALL

Augustine condemned the practice of toasting to someone's health, but only because it was a heathen holdover at the time (it hadn't yet been baptized, so to speak). But maybe Augustine wouldn't mind using his most beautiful passage from the *Confessions* as a preface to a toast:

Late have I loved thee, oh beauty, ever ancient, ever new: late have I loved thee! For behold, you called to me and broke upon my deafness. You sent forth your beams and shone upon me and chased away my blindness. You breathed your fragrance upon me, and I drew in my breath and now pant for

you. I tasted you, and now hunger and thirst for you. I touched
you, and I have burned for your peace.[1]
And through the intercession of St. Augustine, the Doctor
of Grace, may our restless hearts find rest in God.

ST. BARBARA, DECEMBER 4

Because Barbara (fl. third century) was imprisoned by her
cruel father, she is a patron saint of the imprisoned. And
because she converted to Christianity and honored the Trinity by having workers add a third window to her room, she
is a patron saint of architects and builders. But Barbara's
main patronage is due to the way her father died: he was
struck dead by a bolt of lightning not long after executing
his own daughter. Consequently, not only is Barbara invoked
against sudden death and impenitence, but she is a patroness
of everyone who deals with explosives or has any other
extremely dangerous job. Her patronage was extended to
spaces that stored explosives (warehouses and ship holds)
and to those who needed to be very precise, or else ka-boom!
(Think chemical engineers and the like.) And since she was
already protecting the precise, she was made a patroness of
mathematicians.

You could even say that St. Barbara is the patron saint of
barbiturates, since they were named after her thanks to a
strange accident of history. After German chemist Adolf von
Baeyer discovered the substance, he and his colleagues went
to celebrate at a tavern where the local artillery garrison
happened to be celebrating Saint Barbara's Day. When one
of the officers suggested Barbara's name for the new

discovery, Baeyer, his judgment now perhaps softened by a pint or two, agreed. A great discovery, a great saint, and several rounds of merry drinking: these are the stories that warm the cockles of our hearts.

In honor of St. Barbara, mix a Gunfire (see St. Adrian of Nicomedia), a French 75 (see St. Joan of Arc), or an Artillery cocktail.

ARTILLERY

1½ oz. gin
¾ oz. sweet vermouth

1 dash Angostura bitters
1 lemon twist

Pour all ingredients except lemon twist into a mixing glass with ice and stir forty times. Strain into a cocktail glass.

PATRONAGES | Architects, armorers, artillerymen, barbiturates, builders, bomb technicians, brass workers and founders, cannoneers, chemical engineers, fever, fireworks manufacturers, fortifications, gunners, hatmakers, impenitence, mathematicians, military engineers, miners, ordnancemen, prisoners, saltpeter workers, smelters, sudden death, Syria, tilers, tunnellers, U.S. Army Field Artillery, warehouses

LAST CALL

Let us pay tribute to Barbara's patronage of mathematicians with the following toast, loosely inspired by a nineteenth-century toast to the "fair daughters of Maine":

Under the protection of St. Barbara,
May we add virtue to talent,

Subtract envy from friendship,
Multiply accomplishment by humble perseverance,
And divide time by charity.
May the saint help us reach for infinity, and may she teach us to disdain living according to the lowest common denominator.
And of course, may St. Barbara help us with all our math problems and keep us from blowing up.

ST. BÉNÉZET, APRIL 14

Bénézet (ca. 1163–1184) was a shepherd who was told in a vision to build a bridge over the Rhône River at Avignon, France. Everyone refused to help him, and so he built the bridge by himself. When he lifted the huge foundation stone without any help, bystanders shouted, "Miracle! Miracle!" Seventeen more miracles would occur, including making the blind to see, the deaf to hear, the crippled to walk, and the hunchbacks to unhunch. Bénézet's remains made out better than his bridge: the beautiful Pont Saint-Bénézet he completed was partially destroyed by a flood in 1669, yet his body is still incorrupt.

Honor St. Bénézet with any wine from Avignon. The marvelous Châteauneuf-du-Pape would be especially appropriate since the wine is named after the "new" residence of the pope, and one of the titles of the pope is Supreme Pontiff—Latin for "ultimate bridge builder." Or try a *Drinking with Your Patrons Saints* original. The Bridge Builder cocktail includes St. Germain liqueur from Bénézet's native France, and the bourbon, an American creation with a French name, bridges the Old and New Worlds.

BRIDGE BUILDER

1 oz. bourbon
½ oz. St. Germain liqueur
maraschino cherries

½ oz. Aperol
½ oz. lemon juice

Pour all ingredients into a shaker filled with ice and shake forty times. Strain into a cocktail glass. Cut the cherries in half and pierce them with a cocktail spear. Bridge the spear across the rim of the glass.

PATRONAGE | Bridge builders and bridges

LAST CALL

Tonight, build some bridges of your own by inviting over new friends and introducing them to the practice of drinking with the saints.

ST. BERNARD OF MONTJOUX, MAY 28

The archdeacon St. Bernard of Menthon or Montjoux (923–1008) was determined to bring Christianity to the mountain peoples living in the Alps. As part of his evangelization effort and in order to help French and German pilgrims on their arduous trek to Rome, he founded two monasteries and hospices along a pass that crossed the Pennine Alps. One of these was on a treacherous part of the mountain 8,000 feet above sea level, covered year-round with seven to eight feet of snow and with drifts reaching as high as forty feet—oh, and it's susceptible to avalanches in the spring. Bernard's hospices became renowned for their well-trained dogs and brave monks who would scour the area after a storm, rescue those in trouble, and bury those who had perished. And yes, you guessed it: those dogs, which have saved the lives of 2,500 people in the 300 years that their breed has been documented, are now called St. Bernards.

Pope Pius XI made Bernard (the man, not the dog) the patron saint of mountain climbers in 1923. The pope had been a keen climber in his younger days, and he strongly recommended the sport in an Apostolic Letter.

Celebrate St. Bernard with a glass of brandy, preferably served from one of those cute little barrels strapped around a St. Bernard's throat. Or how about a frothy Mountain cocktail?

MOUNTAIN

1¾ oz. rye
¼ oz. dry vermouth
¼ oz. sweet vermouth

¼ oz. fresh lemon juice
1 egg white

Pour all ingredients into a shaker filled with ice and shake forty times. Strain into a cocktail glass.

PATRONAGES | Mountaineers and mountain climbers, inhabitants of and travelers in the Alps

LAST CALL
Throw a mountain-themed party tonight and offer the following toast: "May the prayers of St. Bernard help us climb safely to the top, and may there be a little cask of whisky to greet us when we get there."

ST. BERNARDINE OF SIENA, MAY 20

St. Bernardine (1380–1444) was a Franciscan friar and the greatest preacher of his day, sometimes attracting crowds as large as thirty thousand. The saint initially suffered from hoarseness, but the Blessed Virgin Mary cured him. Bernardine's great cause was promoting devotion to the Holy Name of Jesus, and to this end he invented the *IHS* "logo" (the first three letters of Jesus in Greek). He was also a formidable enemy of vice: when he spoke out against gambling in the city of Bologna, he was so successful that a manufacturer of playing cards went bust. The kind saint, who had a great regard for entrepreneurs, helped the man spring back by suggesting that he print IHS holy cards. The fellow made a small fortune from his newfound piety.

Because of his ability to persuade people of the truth with a few words and telling symbols, Bernardine has become the patron saint of advertisers. And because he was one of the first theologians ever to write an entire work on economics, we recommend him as a patron of economists and entrepreneurs. While we're at it, we also suggest that pious profiteers adopt him as their patron.

Tonight, limit your gambling to a brand-new drink. Andrew Anderson, chief mixologist at Balcones Distilling, has created the Double Down Cocktail just for *Drinking with Your Patron Saints*. Its main ingredient, the magnificent and fiery Balcones Brimstone, will either cure you of hoarseness or cause it.

DOUBLE DOWN COCKTAIL

by Andrew Anderson

1½ oz. Balcones Brimstone   2–3 dashes Angosura bitters
¾ oz. sweet vermouth   1 orange twist
½ oz. Aperol

Build liquid ingredients into an old-fashioned glass filled with ice and stir forty times. Garnish with orange.

PATRONAGES | Advertising and advertisers, against gambling and hoarseness *Suggested Patronages Economists, entrepreneurs, and pious profiteers*

LAST CALL

A toast for our saint: "Through the prayers of St. Bernard, may almighty God increase our love of the Holy Name of Jesus, help us with our business endeavors, and keep us unsullied by deceitful and lewd advertising. And may God bless the drink in our hands, that it may quench our dry throats and put an end to our husky voices."

ST. BLAISE, FEBRUARY 3

Blaise (d. 316) was bishop of Sebaste in historic Armenia (now a part of Turkey). He is one of the Fourteen Holy Helpers and is invoked against diseases of the throat because he once saved a boy choking on a fish bone by praying for him at the request of his desperate mother. And since animals came to him on their own for assistance, he is a patron saint of animals. St. Blaise received the crown of martyrdom when he was tortured with steel wool combs and beheaded for the faith, a manner of death that rendered him a patron of wool combers, weavers, and carvers.

How about honoring St. Blaise with a drink called Down the Hatch?

DOWN THE HATCH

1½ oz. bourbon   2 dashes orange bitters
¾ oz. blackberry brandy

Pour all ingredients into a shaker filled with ice and shake forty times. Strain into a cocktail glass.

PATRONAGES | Animals, carvers, coughs, throat ailments, wool combers, weavers

LAST CALL

Given St. Blaise's protection of the mouth and throat area and his association with fish (or at least its bones), you can add to a cry of "Down the hatch!" an Irish toast: "The health of the salmon to you: a long life, a full heart, and a wet mouth."

Lastly, here is a blessing for the feast of St. Blaise from the *Roman Ritual*:

Blessing of Bread, Wine, Water, Fruit

For the Relief of Throat Ailments on the Feast of St. Blaise

Let us pray.

O God, Savior of the world, who consecrated this day by the martyrdom of blessed Blaise, granting him among other gifts the power of healing all who are afflicted with ailments of the throat; we humbly appeal to Thy boundless mercy, begging that these fruits, bread, wine, and water brought by Thy devoted people be blessed and sanctified by Thy goodness. May those who eat and drink these gifts be fully healed of all ailments of the throat and of all maladies of body and soul, through the prayers and merits of St. Blaise, bishop and martyr.

Amen.

ST. BRIGID, FEBRUARY 1

One of the three patron saints of Ireland, Brigid (451–525) is also invoked for numerous causes. She is the patroness of milkmaids, cattle, and chicken farmers because of her own experience as a slave on a farm; she is a patron saint of babies because she was so well-loved by the Blessed Mother that she was permitted to mystically nurse the Infant Jesus; and she is the patron saint of nuns because of her role in founding religious life in Ireland. But Brigid is also hailed as a patron saint of brewers: in addition to her beautiful prayer "The Lake of Beer," she is said to have turned water into beer in order to quench the thirst of the poor at Easter.

We recommend Irish beer (Guinness, Murphy's, Smith-wick's, and so forth) or any good milk stout to honor our dairy queen. Milk stouts are dark beers brewed with lactose, a type of slightly sweet milk sugar that nicely counterbalances the bitterness of hops and barley.

PATRONAGES | Blacksmiths, cattle, chicken farmers, dairy workers, fugitives, healers, Ireland, milkmaids, nuns, printing presses

LAST CALL
Recite St. Brigid's "Lake of Beer":
I should like a great lake of beer for the King of Kings.
I should like the angels of Heaven to be drinking it through time eternal.
I should like excellent meats of belief and pure piety.
I should like the men of Heaven at my house.
I should like barrels of peace at their disposal.
I should like for them cellars of mercy.
I should like cheerfulness to be their drinking.
I should like Jesus to be there among them.
I should like the three Marys of illustrious renown to be with us.
I should like the people of Heaven, the poor, to be gathered around from all parts.

ST. CADOC, JANUARY 24 (SEPTEMBER 25)

Even before he was born, Cadoc (b. 497) worked miracles. Strange lights shone in his parents' house, and the cellars were miraculously filled with food (hence his patronage of famine victims). Cadoc renounced his royal Welsh lineage to become a monk. He is a patron saint of the deaf because he miraculously healed them. We're not sure why Cadoc is the patron of glandular disorders, but with so many people these days with thyroid problems, why not? They need a divine lobbyist.

Because we tweaked the delicious Red Dragon cocktail by adding an appropriate garnish, we dare to rename it Cadoc's Red Dragon.

CADOC'S RED DRAGON

1 oz. gin   ¾ oz. lemon juice
1 oz. Grand Marnier   1 splash grenadine
¾ oz. blood orange juice   1 cherry

Pour all liquid ingredients into a shaker filled with ice and shake forty times. Strain into an old-fashioned glass with crushed ice and garnish with cherry. For added effect, cut the cherry in half but not all the way; spread out the two connected halves so that it resembles a butterfly, the shape of the thyroid gland.

PATRONAGES | The deaf, famine victims, Glamorgan (Wales), glandular disorders, Llancarfan (Wales), thyroid problems

LAST CALL

A toast: "For the greater glory of God, may St. Cadoc keep our hormones and our spiritual lives well-balanced." And if your guests know how frustrating contemporary thyroid treatment can be, tell them the following joke: "How did they treat hypothyroidism in the old days?" Answer: "Better than they do now!"

St. Cajetan, August 7

Cajetan (1480–1547) was an Italian nobleman who served as a papal diplomat before being ordained a priest. After his ordination, Cajetan used his inheritance to found two hospitals that cared for patients in both body and soul. In 1524 he cofounded the Congregation of Clerks Regular, which is better known as the Theatines because the order began in the Italian city of Chieti, the Latin for which is *Theate*.

Cajetan had an abiding care for the poor. He founded a bank (more like a credit union) to offer an alternative to loan sharks (his bank later became the Banco di Napoli), and he opened up pawn shops called *monts de piété* (mounts of mercy) for the same reason. No one is certain why Cajetan unofficially became a patron saint of gamblers, but it is suspected that many of the people he served through his banks and shops were in debt because of gambling.

Given Cajetan's family wealth as well as his charity on money-related issues, celebrate the saint by enjoying a delicious old-school cocktail called the Millionaire.

Millionaire

2 oz. bourbon
¾ oz. Grand Marnier
½ oz. fresh lemon juice
½ oz. grenadine

¼ oz. absinthe
½ oz. egg white
grated nutmeg

Pour all ingredients into a shaker with no ice and "dry shake" forty times to emulsify the egg. Add ice and shake vigorously for five more seconds. Double-strain into a prechilled champagne coupe glass and garnish with nutmeg.

PATRONAGES | Bankers, gamers and gamblers, good fortune, job seekers, the unemployed, workers

LAST CALL

A toast: "May St. Cajetan, the patron saint of good fortune, keep us always mindful of the less fortunate. And through his intercession, may we be careful what we wish for and obtain what we wish."

ST. CATHERINE OF ALEXANDRIA, NOVEMBER 25

St. Catherine of Alexandria (d. 305) is a popular lady. Because she defeated fifty pagan philosophers in a debate, she is a patroness of several professions or activities involving law or education. Because she was almost executed by a spiked wheel before it was miraculously struck by lightning, she is invoked by anyone remotely connected to wheels or wheel-like devices, including carters, seamstresses, weavers, wool spinners, milliners, and potters. And because she was beheaded, she is invoked against head ailments such as head-aches, migraines, and brain tumors. Finally, because of her virginal marriage to Christ, she is called upon as a protector of purity, a matchmaker for unwed girls, and a patroness of childcare and nurses. Catherine was even occasionally asked to protect against shipwrecks, probably for no other reason than that she had a reputation for powerful intercession. And as if this weren't enough, she is one of the Fourteen Holy Helpers invoked against sudden death.

A "Catherine wheel" is the name for a kind of window in architecture, an embroidery pattern, a rotating firework, and, in Great Britain, a cartwheel. As you mull over those useless facts, sip a Wagon Wheel in honor of St. Catherine.

WAGON WHEEL

1½ oz. Southern Comfort
½ oz. cognac

½ oz. fresh lemon juice
1 dash grenadine

Pour all ingredients into a shaker filled with ice and shake forty times. Strain into a cocktail glass.

PATRONAGES | Apologists, attorneys, brain tumors, carters, childcare, headaches, jurors, knife grinders, librarians and libraries, mechanics, migraines, millers, milliners, notaries, nurses, orators, philosophers, potters, preachers, purity, rope makers, scholars, scribes, seamstresses, students (especially female), sudden death, tailors, theologians, unmarried women, weavers, wheelwrights, wool spinners

LAST CALL

A toast: "May St. Catherine of Alexandria, patroness of many causes, protect us as well as she protected her purity and her faith."

ST. CECILIA, NOVEMBER 22

When St. Cecilia heard profane music at her wedding, she instead "sang in her heart to the Lord alone," making her the patron saint of musicians. On her wedding night, Cecilia revealed to her husband Valerian that she had an angel guarding her virginity. Valerian came to believe her and the two were eventually martyred, Valerian first and later Cecilia. Cecilia was buried at the site of her second-century martyrdom, and when her coffin was opened in 1599 it was revealed, to the amazement of Rome, that her body was still incorrupt.

You can try to make your own body incorrupt tonight by saturating it in alcohol, but it probably won't work. Instead, celebrate St. Cecilia's memory moderately with a glass of vino, such as Planeta's vibrant purplish Santa Cecilia red from Syracuse, Sicily.

PATRONAGES | Musical instruments, musicians, singers, vocalists

LAST CALL

Through the intercession of St. Cecilia, may we sing in our hearts to the Lord alone, and may the music we make with our voices and our instruments reflect that love.

ST. CHRISTOPHER, JULY 25

According to legend, Reprobus was a giant of a man (seven and a half feet tall) from the third century who wanted to serve the greatest king ever. He enlisted in the service of a mighty potentate, but when he noticed that the man was afraid of the Devil, he left him to serve the Prince of Darkness. That did not last long, however: when Reprobus noticed that the Devil was afraid of a roadside cross, he rightly reasoned that Christ was the mightiest of all.

After converting, Reprobus sought the advice of a holy hermit. The hermit told him to fast; Reprobus said he couldn't. The hermit told him to offer many prayers. Ignorant of how to pray, Reprobus again declined. Finally, the hermit suggested that he put his large stature to good use and ferry people across a dangerous river on his shoulders. Incidentally, the hermit is the old man holding the beer on the front cover, ready to reward the saint for his service.

Reprobus happily agreed to the task, and one night he was awakened by a small child asking for passage. As they crossed the river, Reprobus almost collapsed and drowned under the little one's enormous weight. When they reached the other side and the exhausted giant complained, the child replied: "Be not astonished: thou bearest him who beareth the world." As proof, the child commanded Reprobus to plant his staff in the ground, and it blossomed into a palm tree with leaves and dates. Our Lord then baptized Reprobus, changing his name from Reprobus (Latin for "rejected") to Christopher (Greek for "Christ-bearer"). The Christ-bearer went on to suffer martyrdom for his fearless preaching of the Gospel.

Saint Christopher is one of the Fourteen Holy Helpers, a group of saints popular during the Middle Ages for their specific powers of intercession. Christopher was invoked as a patron against sudden death, especially the Plague. There was a rumor going around that anyone who saw an image of the saint would not die suddenly that day. As a result of this belief, images of Saint Christopher were placed near the doors of houses and churches, sometimes on the inside and—for the benefit of passersby—sometimes on the outside. According to one tally, there are more images of Saint Christopher on the walls of old English churches than of any other saint except the Blessed Virgin Mary.

Christopher's job on the river also made him an obvious candidate for patron of ferrymen and their passengers, freight ships and their crews, surfers, sailors, skiers, pilgrims, and travelers. (And because his staff burst into bloom, he was also designated a patron saint of gardeners.) The saint's patronage was extended to motorists in the early twentieth century and caught on quickly, especially since traffic accidents are in some sense the modern plague, taking as many lives as the epidemics of old and in even more sudden a manner. Blessing automobiles on Saint Christopher's Day used to be a common Catholic custom, and Saint Christopher medals or statuettes are still standard on many a Catholic dashboard.

St. Kitts is an island in the Caribbean named after our saint and the home of Brinley Gold rum, which comes in various flavors and is available in the U.S. You can use it to make a Christophe cocktail. Two Belgian breweries have a beer named after St. Christopher: Martens and Brasserie de Silly.

Not far away, Holland's Bierbrouwerij Sint Christoffel makes a number of pilsners and lagers. As for wine, there are several connections to our giant saint. Château Saint-Christophe makes a classic grand cru in the region of Bordeaux. In the Rhône, the AOC appellation (*appellation d'origine contrôlée*) Hermitage was named after a hermitage dedicated to St. Christopher. The Rhône also has an appellation called Plan de Dieu (God's Plan). During the Middle Ages, this area was a forest infested with bandits, and so when you passed through it you were putting your life in God's hands. A fitting wine to commit to your glass on the feast of the patron saint of travelers.

CHRISTOPHE

1½ oz. rum   ¼ tsp. sugar
¾ oz. gin   1 lime wedge

Pour all ingredients except lime into a shaker filled with ice and shake forty times. Strain into a cocktail glass and garnish with lime.

PATRONAGES | Ferrymen and their passengers, freight ships and their crews, gardeners, motorists, pilgrims, sailors, skiers, surfers, travelers ***Suggested Patronages*** *Cab and Uber drivers*

LAST CALL

The French have a saying, often put on their St. Christopher medals, that makes a nice toast: "Look at St. Christopher and go on reassured."

ST. CLARE OF ASSISI, AUGUST 12 (AUGUST 11)

St. Clare (1194–1253) was one of St. Francis of Assisi's first disciples and the foundress of the Order of the Poor Clares. She is the patron saint of embroiderers and related occupations (such as needleworkers, laundry workers, and gilders and goldsmiths) because she spent her years of illness making ornate vestments for use in the sacred liturgy. And in 1958, thanks to Pope Pius XII, she became the patron saint of television, because she saw and heard a Christmas Mass that she was too ill to attend somehow projected on the wall of her room. St. Clare is also a patroness of eye problems—in particular, sore eyes. So the patron saint of television is also the patron saint of sore eyes. Coincidence?

In *Drinking with the Saints* we provided an original concoction using Santa Clara Rompope, a delicious vanilla liqueur from Mexico invented by nuns.

FROZEN CLARISSE

1 cup milk
½ cup Santa Clara Rompope
1½ oz. Kahlúa liqueur

2 cups ice
chocolate syrup

Pour milk, Rompope, Kahlúa, and ice into a blender and blend until smooth. Line the inside of a small snifter glass with chocolate syrup and pour the mix into the glass. Makes approximately four to six 6 oz. servings.

PATRONAGES | Embroiderers, eye problems, gilders and goldsmiths, good weather, laundry workers, needleworkers, television, television actors, workers, writers

> **LAST CALL**
> A toast: "May St. Clare work one of the greatest miracles that can be imagined: keeping us from bad TV."

ST. COMMAN OF IONA, MARCH 18

Talk about a scanty biography. We know that Comman (ca. 688) was the brother of Saint Cumine the White and a monk of Iona Abbey. We also know that the small settlement of Kilchoman on the island of Islay is named after him, and that Kilchoman Distillery, Islay's newest maker of single malt scotch, bears his name. Guess what you're having tonight.

PATRONAGE | None officially except the small settlement on Islay. Comman's brother Cumine the White was more distinguished, so how about making Comman the patron saint of sibling rivalry? We're confident that Comman took his brother's fame in good stride and consoled himself with the knowledge that a fine scotch would carry on his good name.

> **LAST CALL**
> Call an assembly of your "brethren" and offer the following toast: "Through the prayers and example of Saints Comman and Cumine, may the divine gift of fine scotch drown rather than fuel the green-eyed monster of envy and jealousy in our hearts."

ST. DISMAS, MARCH 25

"Dismas" is the name ascribed to the Good Thief, the crucified criminal in the Gospels who refused to join the crowd and mock Jesus but instead asked Our Lord to remember him when He came into His Kingdom. In return, Our Lord promised him that he would see Paradise. According to a charming medieval legend, Dismas had also helped out the Holy Family decades earlier by protecting them from robbers during their flight to Egypt.

A recipe for the Paradise cocktail was first printed by legendary 1920s bartender Harry Craddock and improved over time. We did our test run with the juniper-forward Dripping Springs gin and were pleased with the results. To our booze-addled minds, the name of this gin is evocative of the spring that watered the surface of the earth before God formed man from the slime and placed him in Paradise (Genesis 2:6).

PARADISE

1¼ oz. Dripping Springs gin   ½ oz. orange juice
¾ oz. apricot brandy

Pour all ingredients into a shaker filled with ice and shake forty times. Strain into a cocktail glass.

PATRONAGES | Condemned criminals, theft (against), thieves, undertakers (either because of his peaceful death or because of his loose association with Jesus' funeral)

LAST CALL

Tonight, raise a glass and make the following toast: "To the Good Thief, and through his intercession may we get the nod from our Savior to enter Paradise."

ST. DOROTHY OF CAESAREA, FEBRUARY 6

St. Dorothy (d. 311) is the patroness of brides, midwives, and newlyweds because before she died she was mocked by a pagan who called out, "Bride of Christ, send me some fruits from your bridegroom's garden." She is the patroness of florists and gardeners because she posthumously answered the man's retort by sending a young boy to give him roses and apples, thereby converting him. But Dorothy is also a patron saint of brewers, perhaps because she is sometimes featured in art being burned at the stake, a torture that vaguely recalls the way malt is dried. (For your information, the torture didn't work, and Dorothy was beheaded instead.)

Drink suggestions: A malty beer like a Dogfish Head Raison d'Être, a St. Bernardus Quadrupel, a Trappistes Rochefort, etc. Or enjoy a delicious Jack Rose cocktail, made with apple brandy.

JACK ROSE

2 oz. apple brandy or apple-
jack (we like Laird's)

1 oz. lime juice
½ oz. grenadine

Pour all ingredients into a shaker filled with ice and shake forty times. Strain into a cocktail glass.

PATRONAGES | Brewers, brides, florists, gardeners, midwives, newlyweds

LAST CALL

Have a Dorothy dinner party festooned with roses and apples and kick it off with the following toast: "May Saint Dorothy, a faithful bride of Christ, send us some fruits from her Bridegroom's garden."

ST. DRAUSINUS, MARCH 7

This is definitely a saint you want on your side. Drausinus (d. 674) was the bishop of Soissons, France, who established several religious institutions and persuaded the impious tyrant Ebroin to fund a chapel for sick nuns. But Drausinus is most famous for the legend that spending a night at his tomb renders one invincible. As a result of this tale, entire platoons used to camp out in front of the saint's remains the night before a battle, and St. Thomas Becket visited the tomb before returning to meet his fate in England (we'll assume that "invincibility" here was in reference to St. Thomas's indomitable spirit and not to his impending martyrdom).

Drink suggestion: What else but a Champion Cocktail? Our taste-testing panel feared that with two different kinds of liqueur it would be too sweet, but this well-named concoction stays on top of its ingredients. A true winner.

CHAMPION COCKTAIL

¾ oz. scotch   ½ oz. Bénédictine liqueur
¾ oz. dry vermouth   ½ oz. orange curaçao

Pour all ingredients into a shaker filled with ice and shake forty times. Strain into a cocktail glass.

PATRONAGES | Champions, invincibility, against enemy plots

LAST CALL
Depending on your level of refinement, drink your cocktail as you listen either to Puccini's "Nessun dorma" or to Queen's "We Are the Champions."

ST. DYMPHNA, MAY 15

St. Dymphna, the daughter of a Christian mother and an Irish pagan chieftain, was born sometime in the seventh century. At the death of Dymphna's mother, her father (not to get too clinical here) lost his marbles. When his counsellors advised him to marry again, he said that he would on condition that his new bride was as beautiful as his deceased wife. The only one in the realm who fit that description was Dymphna, and the king, egged on by wicked advisors, had so deteriorated mentally that when he looked at his daughter he only saw her mother. Dymphna fled to Belgium where she built a hospital, but her deranged dad caught up with her and, after she again refused his offer of matrimony, slew her. Understandably, Dymphna is the patron of an array of causes related to mental health and nervous disorders such as epilepsy. She is also invoked against diabolical possession, in the event that a patient's madness is not psychological but demonic. And she is the patron saint of sleepwalkers because of a medieval suspicion that such folk were being nocturnally animated by malign spirits.

Toasts alluding to incest and insanity are not an ideal way to kick off a party, so let's go with the sleepwalker theme and pair our maiden saint with a Sleepy Head. This smooth nightcap adapted from the 1930 *Savoy Cocktail Book* masks the taste of booze so well that you will be nodding off before you know it.

SLEEPY HEAD

1 orange peel
4 fresh mint leaves, crushed

2 oz. brandy
ginger ale

Build orange peel and mint leaves in an old-fashioned glass, crushing the mint leaves. Add brandy and ice and top with ginger ale.[2]

PATRONAGES | Asylums, diabolical possession, epilepsy, incest, the mentally ill, nurses for the mentally ill, nervous disorders, sleepwalking *Suggested Patronage* #MeToo

LAST CALL

A toast: "May St. Dymphna help us keep our heads screwed on straight."

ST. ELIGIUS, DECEMBER 1

St. Eligius (590–660; a.k.a. Eloi or Loy) was an outstanding goldsmith—so outstanding, in fact, that after he was promoted to master of the mint under King Clotaire II of Paris, foreign dignitaries would sometimes visit him before they visited the king. Eligius became wealthy from his trade, but he wore a hair shirt under his gilded finery and generously founded monasteries until he was elected bishop of Noyon-Tournai, even though he was a layman at the time. Because of his skills as a metalworker, Eligius is invoked by a variety of trades involved with metals and gems; and because the saint posthumously healed his old horse for a priest friend who had inherited it, he is a patron of horses and veterinarians. Finally, Eligius is the patron saint of people working in a garage or gas station, which when you think about it is a combination of his two other patronages—of working with metal and with the "horse" of our age.

Did you know that before becoming the title of the best of the Sean Connery James Bond movies, a "goldfinger" was one's ring finger? Neither did we. But we figure the term—and the cocktail named after it—are appropriate for Eligius's heavenly Midas touch. The Goldfinger cocktail has a lovely yellow-golden hue and is ideal as a summer starter or a smooth reminder of summer in the dead of winter.

GOLDFINGER

1½ oz. vodka   ¾ oz. Galliano
1 oz. pineapple juice

Pour ingredients into a shaker filled with ice and shake forty times. Strain into a cocktail glass.

PATRONAGES | Blacksmiths, coin collectors, craftsmen, garage or gas station workers, goldsmiths, horses, jewelers, medal collectors, metalworkers, silversmiths, veterinarians

LAST CALL
"May St. Eligius keep us on the gold standard of orthodox Christianity."

ST. ELMO, JUNE 2

If the name Elmo triggers images of a cloying Muppet, we are happy to infuse your mind with a manlier set of associations. St. Elmo, or Erasmus, was an Italian bishop martyred around AD 303. According to legend, the saint was preaching when lightning suddenly struck the ground next to him; unfazed, he continued his sermon, much to the astonishment of his audience. Elmo's fearlessness became an inspiration for sailors, who soon began to invoke his name when a thunderstorm threatened their ship. They took the harmless corona discharge around the masts of their vessels as an indication that God had heard their prayers. Today that static discharge is known as St. Elmo's Fire.

According to another legend, Elmo (who is one of the Fourteen Holy Helpers) was martyred by having his intestines drawn out and wound around a windlass. It is for this reason that the saint is invoked for intestinal disorders and pains, including those of childbirth.

Drink suggestion: A Salty Dog cocktail (see St. Francis of Paola).

PATRONAGES | Abdominal pains, appendicitis, childbirth, dangers at sea, intestinal disorders, navigators, sailors, seasickness

LAST CALL

A traditional sailor's toast is "Fair winds and following seas," which expresses the wish that your ship will have good winds and favorable waves. Using this nautically rich toast will help dispel the suspicion that you are a pathetic landlubber, and ending it with "through the intercession of St. Elmo" will dupe others into thinking that you are pious.

ST. EXPEDITUS, APRIL 19

Expeditus is said to have been a Roman centurion from Armenia who converted to Christianity and was martyred during the persecution of Diocletian. In Latin, an *expeditus* is an infantryman with no rucksack who can march swiftly, so this may not have been the saint's name but a nickname stemming from his profession. Saints are often "assigned" particular patronages because of puns on their name (or nickname), and Expeditus is a good case in point. He is the patron saint of a speedy end to long legal cases, money issues, and other causes that need immediate resolution; he is also invoked against procrastination. There is a memorable legend to seal his connection to these causes. On the day that Expeditus decided to become a Christian, the Devil took the form of a crow, hopped up to him, and said, "*Cras! cras!*" *Cras* is the Latin version of "caw," but it also means "tomorrow." Thus the Devil was tempting him to put off his embrace of Christ until *mañana*. Expeditus, however, would have none of it. He stamped on the bird and declared, "I'll be a Christian today!"

Old Crow is a bottom-shelf bourbon, but it is better than having to wait until you have saved up enough for something better. And if you have it in a Murder of Crows cocktail you will make the crow-crushing Saint Expeditus proud, even though technically a "murder" refers to a group of crows rather than their massacre.

MURDER OF CROWS

2 oz. Old Crow bourbon
2 oz. orange juice

2 oz. pineapple juice

Pour ingredients into a shaker filled with ice and shake forty times. Strain into a highball glass filled with ice.

PATRONAGES | Money issues, procrastination, speedy cases, urgent causes ***Suggested Patronages*** *Credit cards (He is the patron saint of procrastination and money issues. How fitting for credit cards is that?), social media (since he is the patron saint against wasting time), and expedited shipping*

LAST CALL

The legend of Expeditus reminds us of a great Easter Sunday sermon by St. Augustine of Hippo:

> [I say to the sinner:] "When are you going to reform? When are you going to change?" "*Cras* [Tomorrow]," he says. Look at how much you say *cras, cras*! You have become a crow! Behold, I say to you that when you make the noise of a crow, ruin befalls you. For that crow whose cawing you imitate went forth from the Ark and did not return. Instead, my brother, return to the Church, which the Ark was foreshadowing.

A toast, then, to Saint Expeditus: "Through his intercession, may we never put off until tomorrow what we can do today, and may he help us with all our packages and with all solutions to our problems that absolutely, positively have to be there overnight."

ST. FIACRE, AUGUST 30 (SEPTEMBER 1 IN FRANCE AND IRELAND)

Fiacre of Breuil (d. 670) was an Irish priest who lived in a hermitage in County Kilkenny. Disciples flocked to him, but preferring solitude he moved to what is now Saint-Fiacre, France, and there built an oratory to the Blessed Virgin Mary. When visitors again came knocking on his door, he established a hospice for strangers and served them from his well-kept garden. Fiacre was renowned for his mastery of herbal medicines and had the power of healing by the laying on of hands. An old French word for hemorrhoids is a pun on his name: *le fic* (small tumor) *de S. Fiacre*. Not surprisingly, Fiacre became the patron saint of this asinine condition, as well as of venereal diseases. Some historians claim that the latter patronage is linked to the fact that he would not let women into his hermitage and was therefore considered a misogynist! But we prefer to think that the saint's link to STDs ties in to his reputation as an herbal healer. Less bizarre but more random is his patronage of taxicab drivers. The first taxis in France were located near the Hotel Saint-Fiacre in Paris, and the hackney carriages and later models of taxicabs were subsequently called *fiacres*.

Wine from the Château du Coing de Saint-Fiacre would be great if you can find it—or any herbal liqueur such as Frangelico, Jägermeister, Bénédictine, Chartreuse, or Galliano. Galliano liqueur is made from over thirty herbs and spices, which we can pretend represent Fiacre's garden. A Galliano Sour is an outstanding light and refreshing drink for a garden party; the sourness can symbolize some of Saint Fiacre's distasteful patronages.

GALLIANO SOUR

2 oz. Galliano
1 oz. fresh lemon juice
½ oz. simple syrup

1 dash Angostura bitters
1 egg white (optional)
1 lemon twist

Pour liquid ingredients into a shaker with no ice and "dry shake" forty times to emulsify the egg white, then add ice and shake more. (We recommend the egg white, but if you are making the drink without it, pour all ingredients into a shaker filled with ice and shake forty times.) Strain into an old-fashioned glass filled with crushed ice and garnish with twist.

PATRONAGES | Cab drivers, costermongers (vegetable vendors), fistulas, gardeners, florists, hemorrhoids, horticulturalists, STDs **Suggested Patronages** *Farmers' markets and Uber drivers*

LAST CALL

You can make a toast about hemorrhoids, but it may not sit well with some of your guests. Or you can make a toast about STD testing, but the results may not be positive. Safer is the following toast, adapted from the two traditional blessings of seeds and seedlings for the nearby feast of the Nativity of the Blessed Virgin Mary on September 8: "May the Sower and Cultivator of the heavenly Word who tills the topsoil of our hearts with

spiritual rakes look upon us with merry eyes and a
cheerful countenance: and through the intercession of
Saint Fiacre, may He bless our gardens and our souls, that
both may be free of weeds and full of good fruit."

Final suggestion: Serve some crackers and Brie with your
drinks tonight. Fiacre's Breuil hermitage is in the region of Brie.

St. Fillan, January 9 or August 26

St. Fillan was an Irish hermit who settled in Scotland in
the eighth century. He was a healer of the sick whose left
arm emitted a light that enabled him to study scripture at
night. Centuries later that arm came in handy: King Robert
the Bruce credited his victory over the English at the Battle
of Bannockburn in 1314 to this relic. St. Fillan's Pool was
likewise credited with the power of healing the insane. As
late as the nineteenth century, the mentally ill were dunked
in it in the hopes of a cure and then tied up and left there
overnight; if their bonds came undone by morning, it was a
sign that they had been healed.

A far better alternative to this practice is Macallan single
malt scotch, a smooth and heathery Speyside whisky that
helped put the category of single malt scotch on the map.
And since "Macallan" is Gaelic for "field of Ellan [Fillan],"
you'll be wisely choosing Fillan's field over his pool.

But could this saint of sanity be blessed with *two* scotches
named after him? Possibly. McClelland's Single Malt Highland, Islay, Speyside, and Lowland are four affordable bot-
tlings produced by Morrison Bowmore Distilleries (their

Islay is probably our favorite). And as providence would have it, "McClelland" is Gaelic for "son of the follower of Faolán [Fillan]."

PATRONAGE | The mentally ill

> ### 🔔 LAST CALL
>
> A toast: "May the scotch we drink tonight in honor of St. Fillan be an aid and not an obstacle to our mental health."

ST. FLORIAN, MAY 4

St. Florian (ca. 250) was a Roman soldier whose duties included training an elite group of soldiers to fight fires. Condemned to be burned at the stake for his Christian faith, he egged on the soldiers to light the wood by saying that he would ascend to Heaven on top of the flames. Frightened, the soldiers drowned him instead. Florian's body was recovered, and he went on to become a popular saint in German-speaking areas and the patron saint invoked against dangers from water threatening life or harvest, as well as the patron saint of firefighters and chimney sweeps. To this day, St. Florian's Cross is part of the emblem for fire departments around the world, and in southern Germany and Austria, fire services use the word "Florian" to refer to fire stations and fire trucks.

St. Florian Imperial Red is made by Rust Belt Ale in Youngstown, Ohio, although it is only made from September through December. An easier option is to mix yourself a Fireman's Sour in honor of the patron of firefighters.

FIREMAN'S SOUR

2 oz. lime juice
1 tsp. sugar
½ oz. grenadine

2 oz. light rum
soda water
1 lime wheel and cherry

Pour lime juice, sugar, grenadine, and rum into a shaker filled with ice and shake forty times. Strain into a sour glass, top with soda, and garnish with lime wheel and cherry.

PATRONAGES | Austria, chimney sweeps, firefighters, floods, harvests, Poland, protection in battle, soap boilers, water (against)

LAST CALL
The Florian Principle (Sankt-Florians-Prinzip) is the German equivalent of our "not in my backyard." It is named after a selfish prayer: "O holy Saint Florian, spare my house, kindle others." Try to come up with something a little more charitable as you toast St. Florian, and throw in a good word for firefighters the world over while you're at it.

ST. FOILLAN, OCTOBER 31

St. Foillan (pronounced FWAY-lan and not to be confused with Fillan) was one of an impressive array of Irishmen who evangelized continental Europe in the seventh century.

Foillan worked first in England and then in France, where he founded a monastery. He and his companions were killed by bandits in a forest; Foillan's severed head was still praying out loud when it was thrown into a nearby pigsty (it was later recovered). We're not sure how this charming image makes Foillan the patron saint of children's nurses, but he is.

The Brasserie Saint-Feuillien in Le Roeulx, Belgium, is named after St. Foillan. The brewery makes abbey-style beers, including a much-praised Tripel.

PATRONAGES | Truss makers, dentists, surgeons, children's nurses

LAST CALL

"Through the intercession of St. Foillan, may our children's nurses never give our children nightmares by telling them the story of St. Foillan."

ST. FRANCES OF ROME, MARCH 9

Frances (1384–1440) wanted to become a nun, but her parents arranged a marriage for her at the age of thirteen. Frances loathed conforming to her mother-in-law's socialite expectations, but her husband Lorenzo cared for her deeply and took her side. Frances found a way of balancing her duties as a noblewoman with helping the poor and sick, and she was given the gift of healing. She and Lorenzo had a successful forty-year marriage despite many hardships, including the loss of two children to the Plague, Lorenzo's forced exile, and the confiscation of much of their property when enemy forces conquered Rome.

Frances is an understandable pick for a patroness of widows and the loss of children. She was also chosen by Pope Pius XI to be the patron saint of Roman motorists, possibly because she got around on the darkest of nights with a light from her guardian angel (and we thought halogen headlights were cool). Another good reason is that she frequently drove her wagon around collecting firewood and medicinal herbs for the poor and sick.

The Auto Cocktail was invented in the 1910s, not long after the automobile itself. The recipe calls for Old Tom gin, which is sweeter and less botanically driven than the more common London dry gin. We tried to cheat by using London dry gin, but the result was a bit flat—kind of like using cheap aftermarket parts on your car.

Auto Cocktail

1¼ oz. Old Tom gin   ¾ oz. blended scotch
1¼ oz. dry vermouth   1 lemon twist (optional)

Stir ingredients in a mixing glass with ice until very cold. Strain into a cocktail glass.

PATRONAGES | The death of children (against), the laity, motorists, widows

LAST CALL

Tonight, let the designated driver be named "Saint Frances" and showered with (nonalcoholic) treats and promissory notes for future rounds. Then ask the real Saint Frances for safety on the road, both now and forever, for all present.

ST. FRANCIS DE SALES, JANUARY 29 (JANUARY 24)

Before becoming bishop of Geneva, Switzerland, and help-ing between *forty and seventy thousand* people return to the Catholic faith, Francis de Sales tried to be a dutiful son, secretly studying theology while also practicing fencing and riding to please his rather worldly father. One day while rid-ing, Francis fell three times from his horse, and each time he did his sword and scabbard somersaulted through the air and landed in the shape of a cross. The writing on the wall was clear, and after much disagreement with his father, he was finally ordained a priest.

Francis de Sales was also a tireless educator. He learned sign language just to teach one deaf man about God (he is now a patron saint of the deaf and adult education). But he is perhaps best remembered for his skills as a writer. His *Introduction to the Devout Life* is a spiritual and literary classic eagerly read by Catholic and Protestant alike. As Pope Pius XI put it, Francis argued "forcefully, but with modera-tion and charity." Consequently, the pope declared him patron of all those who "make known Christian wisdom by writing in newspapers or in other journals meant for the general public."

We figure that the tribute to the patron saint of Catholic writers should come from one of them, and so we recom-mend Walker Percy's personal recipe for that great South-ern classic, the Mint Julep. Percy waxed on about this restorative in his delightful 1975 essay "Bourbon." His version saves the sweetness for the bottom of the drink. We would never quibble with an artiste, but if you prefer a more even distribution, substitute one to two teaspoons of simple syrup (equal parts sugar and water) for the dry sugar and stir well before adding the crushed ice.

WALKER PERCY'S PERFECT MINT JULEP

2 oz. "excellent Bourbon whiskey" (Percy liked Early Times Kentucky whiskey)	2 mint sprigs
	crushed ice
	nutmeg, grated
sugar	julep cup or highball glass

"Put half an inch of sugar in the bottom of [an old-fashioned] the glass and merely dampen it with water. Next, very quickly—and here is the trick in the procedure—crush your ice, actually powder it, preferably in a towel with a wooden mallet, so quickly that it remains dry, and, slipping two sprigs of fresh mint against the inside of the glass, cram the ice right to the brim, packing it with your hand. Finally, fill the glass, which apparently has no room left for anything else, with Bourbon, the older the better, and grate a bit of nutmeg on the top. The glass will frost immediately. Then settle back in your chair for half an hour of cumulative bliss."[3]

PATRONAGES | Authors, the deaf, the Catholic press, editors, journalists, writers **Suggested Patronages** *Mediocre equestrians, bargain hunters, and Black Friday (get it?)*

LAST CALL

To help with your writer's block, pour yourself a drink and make the following toast: "May the prayers of St. Francis de Sales, the patron saint of writers, open our hearts to the voice of the Spirit; and may the prayers of St. Francis de Sales, the patron saint of editors, help us dot our i's and cross our t's." Or for a more general occasion, you can say: "Through the intercession of St. Francis, may we never fall on our sword."

ST. FRANCIS OF ASSISI, OCTOBER 4

Giovanni di Pietro di Bernardone (ca. 1181–1226) was nicknamed Francesco—"Frenchy"—by his father, perhaps because of his love of fine clothes. Francis cured himself of this vanity when he exchanged his fancy duds for the rags of a filthy mendicant. For this heroic act, we nominate St. Francis as the patron saint in the race for the cure of metrosexuality.

Francis is better known as a patron saint of animals and the environment. Although he was by no means a vegetarian (he once said that he thought even the walls should enjoy meat on Christmas Day), he was awfully good to the brutes. When the town of Gubbio was being terrorized by a ravenous wolf, St. Francis chastised "Brother Wolf," made the sign of the cross over it, and convinced it to stop killing the townsfolks' livestock. In return, because the wolf had only attacked out of hunger, the saint made the townspeople promise to feed it. The wolf and the citizens of Gubbio became friends from that day on, and they even mourned when the wolf died.

Francis is also the patron saint of numerous cities and dioceses, including the Archdioceses of San Francisco and Santa Fe, both of which are named after him. What, you say? You remember from your high school Spanish that Santa Fe means "Holy Faith" and not "Francis of Assisi"? Quite true, but the original name of New Mexico's capital and the second oldest city in the United States is La Villa Real de la Santa Fe de San Francisco de Asís, that is, the Royal City of the Holy Faith of St. Francis of Assisi. The area was, after all, first evangelized by the Franciscans.

To honor St. Francis's peacemaking skills between man and beast, have a cocktail called the Big Bad Wolf. You can also try a San Francisco, a pleasant dessert drink that has a good balance of flavors and a brilliant vermillion hue. Its key ingredient is sloe gin, a sweet liqueur made from sloeberry or blackthorn plum. You can also try a St. Francis Cocktail, believed to be the prototype of the modern Martini; or just stick to a Martini, since San Franciscans claim that one of their own invented it.

For beer, look no further than the Franziskaner label produced by Spaten-Franziskaner-Bräu in Munich. As for wine, the Franciscan Estate in California's Napa Valley and St. Francis in California's Sonoma County may be Franciscan in name only, but both produce wines that are affordable and good. Or, with a little more effort you can try for a bottle from St. Francis's hometown of Assisi or the region thereof. Assisi is a DOC title in Umbria that includes wineries such as Sportoletti, Falesco, Bodegas Hidalgo, and Legenda.

BIG BAD WOLF

1 oz. brandy
½ oz. orange juice

1 egg yolk
¼ oz. grenadine

Pour all ingredients into a shaker filled with ice and shake forty times. Strain into a cocktail glass.

SAN FRANCISCO

¾ oz. sloe gin
¾ oz. dry vermouth
¾ oz. sweet vermouth

1 dash orange bitters
1 dash Angostura bitters
1 cherry for garnish (optional)

Pour ingredients into shaker filled with ice and shake forty times. Strain into a cocktail glass and garnish with cherry.

ST. FRANCIS COCKTAIL

2 oz. gin
1 dash vermouth

1 dash orange bitters
olives

Pour liquid ingredients into a mixing glass with ice and stir forty times. Strain into a cocktail glass and garnish with olives.

MARTINI

2 oz. gin
1 dash dry vermouth

1 lemon twist or olives

Pour liquid ingredients into a mixing glass with ice and stir forty times. Strain into a cocktail glass and garnish with olives or twist.

PATRONAGES | Animal welfare societies, animals, Archdioceses of San Francisco and Santa Fe, ecologists, environment, families, Italy, merchants, tapestry workers, zoos **Suggested Patronages** Metrosexuality (against)

LAST CALL

St. Francis of Assisi used to call his body "Brother Ass." Like any jackass or jennyass, the body sometimes needs a stick and sometimes a carrot, and sometimes even a sugar cube. Tonight, give Brother Ass the sugar cube.

ST. FRANCIS OF PAOLA, APRIL 2

Francis of Paola (1416–1507) was the founder of the Order of Minims. He had the gift of prophecy and the ability to read consciences. In France, he is remembered for a gift that he brought to King Louis XI from his native home of Calabria, Italy: Bartlett pears. The saint's nickname at court was *le Bon Chrétien* or "the Good Christian," and this moniker was applied to the pear he had introduced to the country. To this day, what is called a Bartlett pear in the U.S. and a Williams pear in Great Britain is known in France as a *poire bon chrétien.*

The profile of the Good Christian also appears on the neck of every bottle of Paulaner beer, which was established in the seventeenth century by the Minim friars and named after their order's founder. (The monastery was eventually closed and the beer production taken over by a secular company.)

But Francis's patronages stem from a single miracle that he once performed. In 1464, Francis crossed the Strait of

Messina to Sicily by laying his cloak on the water, tying one end to his staff to make a sail, and then sailing across the sea with his companions. At the height of World War II (1943), Pope Pius XII made the saint's patronage of naval officers and navigators official.

Drink suggestions: Paulaner beer, pear liqueur, or a Salty Dog, a mixed drink bearing the nautical nickname for an experienced sailor. Or have a go at Navy Strength gin: we like Vigilant's, which is made with fig, hops, orris root, and hibiscus, and Fords Gin Officers' Reserve. Navy Strength is a high-proof gin (114 or above!)—and the reason that we speak of a liquor's concentration of alcohol in terms of "proof": In the days when sailors were paid partly in gin rations, suspicious sailors would test the strength of their rations by mixing some of the gin with gunpowder and lighting it. If it ignited, it was "proofed" and not watered down. Navy Strength gin could also be spilled in the hold without ruining the gunpowder.

A Gimlet is an ideal way to enjoy Navy Strength gin, especially because it originated in the merchant navy as a nice way to use up old limes and prevent scurvy.

SALTY DOG

1½ oz. vodka
grapefruit juice (Ruby Red for
  a sweeter flavor)

1 lime slice (optional)
Salt for rimming (optional)

Build ingredients in a highball glass filled with ice. If you want the glass rimmed with salt, first moisten the rim of the glass with water and dip it in a ring of salt.

GIMLET

1½ oz gin   1 tsp. powdered sugar
1 oz. lime juice

Pour all ingredients into a shaker filled with ice and shake forty times. Strain into a cocktail glass. Note: For an added treat, rim the glass with sugar (powdered or granulated) beforehand.

PATRONAGES | Naval officers, navigators, sailors, and all those associated with the sea *Suggested Patronage Windsurfing*

LAST CALL

Steal the sailor's toast from St. Elmo or try the following: "With the help of St. Francis of Paola, may our lives and the lives of those at sea be smooth sailing."

ST. GALL, OCTOBER 16

No one is certain why the Irish-born monk and missionary St. Gall (d. 635) is the patron saint of birds. Is it because *gallo* is the Italian word for rooster? Or is it because of the time that he exorcised a demon from a girl and the demon escaped through the girl's mouth in the form of a blackbird? Either way, the canton of St. Gallen in Switzerland is named after this popular preacher who evangelized the region. Even bears respected him. When St. Gall, travelling in the woods, was warming his hands over a campfire, a bear emerged from the darkness and charged. The holy Irishman, however, rebuked the bear, which slunk away to gather firewood and then returned to join him at the fire. The bear never left his side after that.

Drink suggestions: Find a drink with a volucrine association. Options include but are not limited to:

For beer: Goose Island Beer Co. (Chicago), Kingfisher, RavenBeer from Baltimore, Old Speckled Hen, and Rushing Duck brewery in Hudson Valley, New York.

For liquor: Eagle Rare Fighting Cock bourbon, Old Crow bourbon, Famous Grouse scotch (a best-value buy), Grey Goose vodka, Redbreast Irish whiskey (one of our favorites!), Wild Turkey, and Woodcock Pennsylvania Straight Rye Whiskey.

For wine: Baby Duck, Cold Duck, Covey Run, Duckhorn's Canvasback Cabernet Sauvignon, Eye of the Swan, Hawk Crest, Lamothe Parrot Wine, Ravenswood, Red Rooster, Rex Goliath, Screaming Eagle, Smoking Loon, Thirsty Owl vineyards in the Finger Lakes region, Thunderbird (a bottom-shelf fortified wine), and Winking Owl at a whopping three dollars a bottle.

PATRONAGE | Birds *Suggested Patronage* Bear attacks

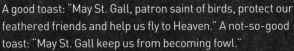

LAST CALL

A good toast: "May St. Gall, patron saint of birds, protect our feathered friends and help us fly to Heaven." A not-so-good toast: "May St. Gall keep us from becoming fowl."
Final suggestion: Host a wine and cheese party and serve St. Gall, an award-winning wheel-shaped hard cheese made from the milk of Friesian cows.

ST. GEORGE, APRIL 23

St. George's dramatic defeat of a dragon that was terrorizing a town has made him the patron of numerous causes. As one of the Fourteen Holy Helpers, George is asked to protect domestic animals; as a resourceful outdoorsman, he is a patron of the Boy Scouts and, more recently, the Catholic Troops of Saint George; and as a mounted knight he is the patron of two knightly orders, of horsemen and things pertaining to them (such as saddle-making), of several cavalries (including modern tank divisions), and of various wielders of swords and knives, including butchers. But why is St. George invoked against herpes and syphilis? Perhaps because as a patron of soldiers, he is invoked against diseases brought about by soldiers' vices.

To celebrate St. George, try a wine or vodka from Georgia—not the American state, but the Eurasian country—or anything from St. George's Distillery in England, such as the fortified wine St. George's Pedro Ximénez. Or how about a satisfying St. George cocktail?

ST. GEORGE

1½ oz. Hendrick's gin
½ oz. dry vermouth
1 dash lime juice

3 olives stuffed with bleu cheese

Pour gin, vermouth, and lime juice into a shaker filled with ice and shake forty times. Strain shaker into cocktail glass and garnish with olives on a spear—which, of course, represents St. George lancing the dragon.

PATRONAGES | Armorers, Boy Scouts, butchers, chivalry, domestic animals, England, Ethiopia, farmers, Georgia, herpes and syphilis (against), horsemen, leprosy, Order of Teutonic Knights, Order of the Garter, Palestinian Christians, saddlers, soldiers, Troops of Saint George, U.S. Army Cavalry, U.S. Marine Corps

LAST CALL

English armies once used the saint's name as a battle cry, shouting "Montjoie! Saint George!" (A *montjoie* was a standard that showed the troops the way into battle.) Tonight, raise your glass, harness the gusto of a drill sergeant, and boom out: "May St. George help us to slay the dragons in our lives. Montjoie! Saint George!"

ST. GERTRUDE OF NIVELLES, MARCH 17

When she was ten years old, the king asked St. Gertrude (626–659) if she would like to marry the son of a duke. The little spitfire "lost her temper and flatly rejected him with an oath, saying that she would have neither him nor any earthly spouse but Christ the Lord." Gertrude's wish came true when at the age of twenty she was made abbess of the monastery at Nivelles in Belgium. She actively supported the missions of Irish monks like St. Foillan. Because she built hospices for pilgrims, she came to be seen as a patron saint not only of travelers but of the deceased journeying into the next world. Teutonic imagination associated souls with mice and rats, and thus she was portrayed with these critters running up and down her staff. But when the original symbolism was forgotten, Gertrude came to be seen as a protectress *against* mice and rats. And if she is against mice and rats, then clearly she is for cats, yes? Sure enough, within the last few decades she has unofficially become their patron saint as well.

Appropriately, this supporter of Irish missionaries died peacefully on St. Patrick's Day in 659. Gardeners consider fine weather on her feast day as a good sign to begin spring planting. Gertrude is also a patroness of the mentally ill, either because her patronage of gardens associates her with healing or because she patronizes cat owners (just kidding!) Then again, there are no stereotypical crazy *dog* ladies, are there?

Finally, Gertrude is a patron saint of travelers because, according to legend, when a large sea monster threatened to capsize the ship of an underling she had sent on a trip, he called out to her and the slimy beast immediately slunk away. In memory of this event, medieval travelers drank so-called Sinte Geerts Minne (St. Gertrude's Love) or Gertrudenminte before hitting the road. We bet you didn't know that the technical term for this kind of parting glass is called a "stirrup cup," a "cup of wine or other drink handed to a man when already on horseback setting out for a journey." You can even purchase metal "stirrup cups" (usually hunting-themed) that are designed "to fit a hand on the go."

Unless, of course, you're about to get behind the wheel, this is a tradition that cries out for retrieval. Port and sherry are old English favorites for the stirrup cup, but you can honor St. Gertrude's Love with whatever beverage you wish. Better yet, here's a 1937 cocktail with the right name for the job that is delightfully light and refreshing.

STIRRUP CUP

1½ oz. brandy
1½ oz. Cherry Heering
1 tsp. sugar

½ oz. fresh lemon juice
1 maraschino cherry

Dissolve the sugar in a little bit of water at the bottom of a cocktail shaker or mixing glass. Add the lemon juice and the two brandies. Add crushed ice and stir well. Strain into a cocktail glass and drop in the cherry.

PATRONAGES | Cats, gardeners, the mentally ill, mice and rats, travelers

LAST CALL

Come up with clever ways of combining all of Gertrude's patronages for a party, such as an Irish mouse dressed for a funeral and carrying flowers about to mount a horse. We're confident that you'll get nothing but approving looks from any baker you ask to put that image on a cake. And be sure to accompany every round, especially the last one, with the following toast: "To the love of St. Gertrude: may it protect us from all harm on all of our journeys."

ST. GILES, SEPTEMBER 1

St. Giles, a.k.a. Aegidius (650–710), is one of the Fourteen Holy Helpers. He is invoked against plague, for a good confession, and for cripples, beggars, and blacksmiths. A native of Athens, Giles sought the life of a hermit and moved to a cave in the woods of France (hence his patronage of forests). God favored his choice, sending him a red doe each day that gave him her milk. All was well until a king and his friends were hunting and chased the deer into Giles's cave. One of them shot an arrow into the cave, wounding Giles in the leg and permanently maiming him (hence his patronage of cripples and the lame). The king felt awfully bad about the incident; he eventually founded a great monastery and made Giles its abbot. The town of Saint-Gilles-du-Gard grew up around the monastery, and Giles's tomb became a pilgrimage site for women struggling with infertility.

Because cripples often found themselves begging on the street, Giles also became a patron of beggars, lepers, the poor and outcast, and all the physically handicapped. And because of his daily diet of deer milk, he became a patron of breastfeeding. But if one is interceding on behalf of breastfeeding, why stop there? Thus Giles is also invoked against breast cancer. And people wishing to make a good confession turn to Giles because of an anachronistic legend involving Charlemagne (who was born thirty-two years after the saint's death). According to the story, Giles was about to pardon the emperor's sins when an angel dropped a letter on the altar outlining a terrible sin that Charlemagne dared not confess. Finally, we don't know why Giles is invoked against "childhood fears" such as noctiphobia (fear of the night), unless perhaps it is because Giles was not afraid of living in a dark cave in a dark wood.

If Saint Giles can get milk from a doe, we can get scotch from a stag, specifically the one on every label of Glenfiddich single malt scotch. "Glenfiddich," it so happens, is Gaelic for "valley of the deer." Or, in honor of the monastery he founded, enjoy some Mannochmore, a single malt Speyside scotch with a name that means "the great place of the monks."

St. Giles's symbol is an arrow, but you can avoid the shaft and get straight to the point with an Arrowhead Cocktail. With an ounce of lemon juice, this drink is appropriately sharp but good.

ARROWHEAD COCKTAIL

1 egg white
1 oz. whisky
¼ oz. sweet vermouth

¼ oz. dry vermouth
1 oz. fresh lemon juice

Pour all ingredients into a shaker filled with ice and shake forty times. Strain into a cocktail glass.

PATRONAGES | Beggars, blacksmiths, breast cancer (against), breastfeeding, confession, cripples, fear of night (against), forests, the handicapped, hermits, infertility (against), the lame, lepers, the poor, the outcast, rams, spur makers **Suggested Patronages** Deer and survivalists

LAST CALL

Tonight, overcome your fear of the dark or of being an outcast and give the following lame toast: "To St. Giles, the holy hermit who was nursed by a deer: may he forever fawn over us from Heaven."

ST. GUMMARUS, OCTOBER 11

The Belgian saint Gummarus (717–744) was happy serving at the court of King Pepin until he got married. His wife Guinimaria was described as "extravagant and perverse in her ways, cruel, capricious and altogether unteachable." Gummarus strove, through soft degrees, to make his wife agreeable to reason and religion, but he was called away to war for eight years. When he returned, he found the place in shambles thanks to Guinimaria's cruelty and incompetence. Apparently, "She was so mean that she even refused beer to the reapers at harvest!"[4] Gummarus made full restitution to the servants and tenants she had wronged (which is why, we suspect, he is the patron of cowherds and so forth), and his good example even affected Guinimaria for a while. However, her good behavior did not last long and she soon reverted to her old ways. (Could her painful presence also be why Gummarus is invoked against hernias?) In any event, Gummarus finally gave up and, along with St. Romuold, founded an abbey at Lierre.

Make sure that you give your reapers beer at harvest. The microbrewery Sint Jozef in Belgium makes a Sint-Gummarus beer. In the U.S., Austin Beerworks, the Kelsen Brewing Company, and the Buxton Brewery all make a Battle Axe beer or ale: the name evokes St. Gummarus's association with wood choppers, and it is an indirect reminder of Guinimaria's behavior. If you can't find these brews, restrain your inner Guinimaria and calmly find a substitute of your choosing.

PATRONAGES | Childless people, courtiers, cowherds, difficult marriages, foresters, glove makers, hernias, lumberjacks, separated spouses, woodcutters

LAST CALL

Today, be extra nice to your spouse as you recall Shakespeare's ominous line: "Better well-hanged than ill-wed." Then, offer the following toast: "May the prayers of St. Gummarus keep us from the marital life of St. Gummarus, and may our harvest reapers and other such folk never want for beer."

ST. HELEN, AUGUST 18

Helen, or Helena, (ca. 250–330) was the mother of Constantine, the Roman emperor who ended the imperial persecution of Christianity. Helen was an old woman when she journeyed to the Holy Land and, with considerable energy and discernment, completed the arduous task of finding the True Cross. Because of her success, she is an unofficial patroness of archeologists and new discoveries.

Drink suggestions: The wines of Santa Helena from Chile or a *Drinking with your Patron Saints* original cocktail. The Truly Crossed contains fragrant and delicious lavender. According to one enthusiast, "When we use lavender . . . we receive the blessings of the feminine," a fit reminder of Helen's maternal protection.

TRULY CROSSED

by Alexandra Foley

1½ oz. Tito's vodka
1 tbsp. Monin's lavender syrup
1 tbsp. fresh lemon juice

1 dash of lemon bitters or lemon essential oil (optional)

Pour ingredients into a shaker filled with ice and shake forty times. Strain into a cocktail glass and garnish with orange twist.

PATRONAGES | Archeologists, new discoveries

LAST CALL

In his wonderful novel *Helena*, Evelyn Waugh has our saint proclaim: "You can't just send for Peace and Wisdom, can you? Why, they don't exist at all except *in people*, do they? Give me real bones every time."[5] A toast, then, in honor of St. Helen: "May our excavations yield real bones and our hearts peace and wisdom."

ST. HOMOBONUS, NOVEMBER 13

Homobonus lived up to his name, which literally means "good man." Born in Lombardy, Homobonus was an honest, orderly, and generous merchant, looking upon the care of his business as a duty given to him by God. The good man also served the poor, going to their homes, tending to their needs, and exhorting them to a better life. He died while attending Mass, stretching out his arms in the figure of a cross during the "Gloria in excelsis" and falling face forward to the ground. (When he didn't stand up for the Gospel, people figured out that something was wrong.) Since Homobonus already had a few miracles to his credit, he was canonized in 1199, only two years after his death.

Not all goody-goodies are insufferable, such as this outstanding cocktail from 1937.

GOODY-GOODY

by G. Bongarzoni
1½ oz. Booth's gin
¾ oz. red Dubonnet
½ oz. fresh lemon juice

½ oz. yellow Chartreuse
1 orange twist (optional)

Pour liquid ingredients into a shaker filled with ice and shake forty times. Strain into a cocktail glass and garnish with orange twist.

PATRONAGES | Businessmen, clothworkers, garment workers, merchants, shoemakers, tailors, tradesmen

LAST CALL

A toast: "May God bless our businesses and our professional activities, and through the intercession of St. Homobonus may a good man not be hard to find in our lives or in the mirror."

ST. HONORATUS OF AMIENS, MAY 16

Honoratus, the seventh bishop of Amiens, France (who is not to be confused with Honoratus of Lérins), is the patron saint of bakers, cake makers, and the related occupations of millers, oil refiners, and so forth. According to one theory, Honoratus was such a hellion in his youth that his old nursemaid, who was making bread when she heard he had been consecrated bishop, refused to believe the news unless her peel—the giant wooden spatulas used to slide pizzas and loaves of bread in and out of the oven—sprouted roots and grew into a tree (which it did). According to another theory, the patronage is due to the fact that once while Honoratus was celebrating Mass, our Lord took the Host from the saint's hands and gave him Holy Communion.

Honoratus means "honored" in Latin. The Honorable
Cocktail is essentially a variation of a Perfect Manhattan:
whether that makes it an Imperfect Manhattan or a Plu-
perfect Manhattan we leave to your discretion. In any
event, we suggest adding a twist of lemon to the Honorable
to complete the effect: you can tell your guests that the
lemon peel symbolizes the nursemaid's peel that turned
into a tree.

HONORABLE COCKTAIL

1½ oz. bourbon   ½ oz. sweet vermouth
½ oz. dry vermouth   1 lemon twist (optional)

Pour ingredients into a mixing glass with ice and stir forty times.
Strain into a cocktail glass and garnish with lemon twist. (N.B.:
We're normally broad-minded about shaking vs. stirring, but the
stirred version of this drink is definitely better, since shaking
waters it down too much.)

PATRONAGES | Bakers, chandlers, confectioners,
flour merchants, millers, oil refiners, pastry chefs

LAST CALL

Before dinner, enjoy an Honorable Cocktail; after dinner,
treat yourself to a St. Honoré cake, a delicious pastry
honoring today's saint. There is a good recipe for it in Ernst
Schuegraf's *Cooking with the Saints*.

ST. HUBERT OF LIEGE, NOVEMBER 3

Hubert (656–727) is the patron saint of hunters, archers, and trappers because he is said to have had a religious conversion while hunting on Good Friday: He saw a glowing cross between a stag's antlers and heard a voice telling him to change his ways or go to Hell. Hubert obliged and became bishop of Liege. As a hunter, Hubert is associated with dogs and is invoked against rabies. To this day in Catholic Europe, the hunting season is formally begun with a Mass on St. Hubert's Day to which the hounds are brought. During the elevation of the Host and Precious Blood, the hunters, resplendent in their green and red hunting jackets, sound their horns; after the Mass, the priest blesses St. Hubert's Bread, Water, and Salt specifically against rabies and gives them to the hounds. Finally, there is a legend about St. Peter giving Hubert a special key to guard against evil spirits. "St. Hubert's Keys" (often in the shape of nails, crosses, or cones) were used against rabies; when heated and placed on a fresh bite they cauterized the wound and killed the rabies virus. We suspect that St. Hubert became the patron of metalworkers and the like because of his association with this charm; maybe precision instrument makers and opticians were put under his mantle for this reason as well. And like St. Barbara, once he patronized precision, his patronage of mathematicians was only natural.

Drink suggestions: For wine, something from Argentina's Bodegas San Huberto. For liqueur, the famous Jägermeister is German for "master of the hunt" and features St. Hubert's stag on every bottle. For cocktails, go for a Hart—the word for a red male deer at least five years old—or a Hunter. For added symbolism (and to save some money), use Hunter Rye, an inexpensive Canadian whisky imported and blended by the Sazerac Company in Kentucky. It works as well in a Manhattan as in a Hunter cocktail, though don't forget that it weighs in at 90 proof. For something higher on the shelf, one can never go wrong with Basil Hayden's Dark Rye, a masterful blend of Kentucky and Canadian rye with a touch of California port. And it doesn't hurt that Basil Hayden Sr., after whom the rye is named, built the first Catholic chapel on the Kentucky frontier.

HART

1 oz. gin	1 oz. dry vermouth
1 oz. red Dubonnet	

Pour ingredients into a mixing glass with ice and stir forty times. Strain into a cocktail glass.

HUNTER

1½ oz. rye whiskey	1 maraschino cherry (optional)
¾ oz. cherry brandy (kirsch)	

Pour liquid ingredients into a mixing glass with ice and stir forty times. Strain into a cocktail glass. We recommend adding a maraschino cherry for garnish; it balances the drink nicely, and a speared cherry is a good symbol for a holy hunter whose heart was pierced with compunction—and for archers and bowhunters in general.

PATRONAGES | Archers, dogs, hunters, machinists, mathematicians, metalworkers, opticians, precision instrument makers, rabies, smelters, trappers

LAST CALL

Stirrup cups (as explained in the entry for St. Gertrude above) were a popular tradition with European hunters. Tonight, lift high your own stirrup cup as you ask God, by way of a toast, to grant you happy hunting through the help of Saint Hubert. We also found an old English toast to which we added a reference to St. Hubert:

To the love of our patron Saint Hubert!
Horses sound, dogs healthy;
Earths stopped, foxes plenty.

(You can substitute something on your list of quarry for anything in the toast. For example, you can say "ATVs" instead of "horses," and "whitetail" or "mule deer" instead of "foxes.")

And if you are invoking Hubert not for his hunting prowess but for his penchant for precision, take the toast to St. Barbara above and repurpose it.

St. Isidore of Seville, April 4

Isidore of Seville (560–636) is a Doctor of the Church and the "last scholar of the ancient world," but he did not start out that way. A poor student, he eventually put his entire trust in God and went on to become the most learned man of his day, carefully preserving all the ancient learning he could and successfully synthesizing the remnants of Roman civilization with the ascendant Visigothic culture of ancient Spain. Isidore is best known for his *Etymologies*, a fascinating (and sometimes fantastic) encyclopedia that in some respects is the world's first database of knowledge. Consequently, Isidore is considered the patron saint of computers and the internet, even though the Magisterium has not issued any official decrees.

The Master of Malt distillery makes a high-end Saint Isidore blended scotch whisky that is difficult to find in the U.S. but can be purchased online. We're not sure, though, that St. Isidore would appreciate his likeness on the label. A simpler option is to celebrate a drink from Isidore's adopted town of Seville: the Tinto de Verano, a sangria-like drink popular among Sevillanos.

TINTO DE VERANO

1½ oz. red wine   3 lemon wedges
lemon-lime soda

Put lemon wedges into a highball glass, fill with ice cubes, and add red wine. Top with soda.

PATRONAGES | Computer programmers, computer scientists, computers, the internet, IT support, and software developers ***Suggested Patronage*** *Entryways (get it?)*

LAST CALL

Father John T. Zuhlsdorf has written a lovely prayer for Isidore:

> Almighty and eternal God, who hast created us in Thy image and bade us to seek after all that is good, true, and beautiful, especially in the divine person of Thy only-begotten Son, our Lord Jesus Christ: grant, we beseech Thee, that through the intercession of Saint Isidore, bishop and doctor, during our journeys through the internet, we will direct our hands and eyes only to that which is pleasing to Thee and treat with charity and patience all those whom we encounter. Through Christ our Lord. Amen.

St. Ivo of Kermartin, May 19

Brittany's St. Ivo, or Yves, (1253–1303) studied canon and civil law before becoming a judge conspicuous for his integrity, wisdom, and care for the poor and orphaned. Ivo was eventually ordained a priest, but he continued to practice law. Once, when a mother and son could not resolve their differences, Ivo offered a Mass for them, and they immediately reconciled. Ivo was eventually made a pastor of two different parishes. As far as we can tell, he is the only parish priest from the Middle Ages to be canonized.

To honor an advocate after Solomon's own heart, have a Judge Jr. cocktail. We don't know why this excellent cocktail is so named, but if this is the junior version, we'd love to meet the senior.

JUDGE JR.

¾ oz. gin   ½ oz. fresh lemon juice
¾ oz. light rum   ½ oz. grenadine

Pour ingredients into a shaker filled with ice and shake forty times. Strain into a cocktail glass.

PATRONAGES | Abandoned children, advocates, canon lawyers, judges, lawyers, notaries, orphans

LAST CALL

A toast for lawyers: "Through the intercession of Saint Ivo, may we choose justice over victory, integrity over lucre, and truth over persuasion: that we may defend the widows and orphans of our age."

A toast for non-lawyers: "May Saint Ivo protect us from ambulance chasers and other shysters."

A toast for everyone, from the Anglo-Irish poet Richard Brinsley Butler Sheridan (1751–1816):

A bumper of good liquor
Will end a contest quicker
Than justice, judge, or vicar.
So fill a cheerful glass
And let good humor pass.

Of course, a bumper of good liquor can *start* a contest quickly as well, but we'll focus on the positive.

ST. JOAN OF ARC, MAY 30

The "Maid of Orléans" (1412–1431) was a French peasant who, at the age of thirteen, was told in a vision involving Saints Michael, Catherine of Alexandria, and Margaret of Antioch to drive out the English and bring Charles VII to Reims for his coronation. Voices from above persisted, and she gradually learned that she was being called to lead the French army, even though she herself never fought in the battles. She was also guided by these voices to find an ancient sword buried behind the altar of a chapel.

After successfully completing her military mission, St. Joan was captured by the Burgundians, betrayed to the English, put on trial for heresy, and burned at the stake at the age of nineteen. Twenty-five years later, however, Pope Calixtus III declared her innocent of the charges. She was canonized in 1920 and made one of the patron saints of France.

St. Joan's hometown of Orléans is in the Loire wine-making region of France. There is an Orléans AOC appellation for various red, white, and rosé wines as well as an Orléans-Cléry AOC appellation. You can also make the region of Burgundy pay for their perfidious abduction of the saint by providing the wine for tonight.

Or, have a swank French 75, an outstanding cocktail developed during World War I that was said to have the kick of the powerful French 75 mm field gun. True, it was not St. Joan's weapon of choice, but French soldiers did carry her image into the trenches of the Great War, and we're confident some of those images found their way onto a French 75.

FRENCH 75

1½ oz. gin
½ oz. lemon juice
2 tsp. simple syrup

5 oz. brut champagne
lemon twist, cherry, orange
slice (optional garnishes)

Pour gin, lemon juice, and simple syrup into a shaker filled with ice and shake forty times. Strain into a champagne flute or champagne tulip and top with champagne. Garnish with lemon or cherry, or both, and orange slice.

PATRONAGES | Captives, France, prisoners, soldiers, the opposition of Church authorities **Suggested Patronages** *Scavenger hunts, at least those involving buried swords*

LAST CALL

A toast to Saint Joan: "May she increase the faith in France, defend all wrongly accused by Church authorities, console all prisoners, protect all soldiers, and give us all brave hearts. And while she's at it, may she help us find buried treasure."

ST. JOHN BOSCO, JANUARY 31

"Don Bosco" (1815–1888) was the founder of the Salesian Order who worked tirelessly with street children and juvenile delinquents. The kindhearted saint often used magic tricks to attract the attention of these underprivileged youths and then teach them about God or take them to Mass. St. John Bosco also pioneered a pedagogy of love rather than punishment, later known as the

Salesian Preventive System. In 1946 Pope Pius XII declared Don Bosco a patron of Catholic editors for his authorship of highly popular religious books and for replacing suspect passages in non-Catholic books with acceptable Catholic statements.

To honor Don Bosco's work with children through magic tricks, have fun with a Magic Cotton Candy Daiquiri Cocktail. In terms of presentation, it tops the list of drinks in this book. Supermarkets occasionally sell cotton candy and you can also make your own or order online, but your best bet is to find a good candy store—and pick up an extra treat for yourself while you're there.

MAGIC COTTON CANDY DAIQUIRI COCKTAIL

2 oz. light rum
juice of 1 lime (2 tbsp.)
champagne

cotton candy
1 lime wheel

Place a big fluff of cotton candy in a cocktail glass. Pour rum and lime juice into a shaker filled with ice and shake forty times. Strain into the cocktail glass, "magically" dissolving the cotton candy. Top with champagne and garnish with a lime wheel.

PATRONAGES | Apprentices, editors, juvenile delinquents, magicians, Mexican youth (by decree of the Holy See in 1935), publishers, schoolchildren, youth

LAST CALL

A toast: "May the prayers and example of St. John Bosco fill our hearts with a magical wonder and love for God—and keep our kids out of juvie."

ST. JOHN MARY VIANNEY, AUGUST 9 (AUGUST 4)

John Mary Vianney (1786–1859) almost did not become a priest. His Latin scores were terribly low, and just when he was nearing ordination he was conscripted into Napoleon's Grande Armée. His company was deployed, but Vianney's poor health prevented him from joining them, and when he tried to catch up to them, he collapsed in a forest. Now considered a deserter, the frail seminarian went on the lam. Once, a searcher thrust a bayonet into the haystack in which he was hiding; the bayonet pierced him, but he made no sound.

It's a good thing that he persisted. After he became the pastor—or curé—of Ars, John Mary not only transformed the tiny French village of 253 people but enriched the entire Church. An indefatigable priest who spent up to sixteen hours a day in the confessional, he had the gift of reading people's hearts and was frequently harassed by the Devil, who was not pleased with the saint's success.

John Mary Vianney had a gentle heart, except where dancing was concerned. The best explanation we found of the saint's strict policy against even watching others dance is the one offered by Mary Reed Newland:

> The people of Ars did not do the stately ga-
> votte or minuet but the bourrée, a polka-like

step which, fueled by hearty drinking, degen-
erated into a rustic bacchanale after which the
couples drifted off to the hedges—and nine
months later saw the inevitable results.[6]

Now we get it! And so we hereby dub St. John Mary
Vianney the patron saint to be invoked against dirty
dancing as well as the patron saint of Southern Baptists,
who should appreciate not only the holy man's opposition
to dancing but the fact that his sermons on moderation
drove four local taverns out of business.

The Curé d'Ars is also the patron saint of the Archdiocese of Dubuque, Iowa, and we think we know why.
Because he struggled academically, Vianney was tutored
by a seminary classmate named Mathias Loras. One day,
Loras grew so frustrated with his pupil's lack of progress
that he struck him. In response, John Mary fell to his knees
and asked for forgiveness. You can imagine what a cad
Loras felt like then. He immediately embraced John Mary
and they became fast friends from that day on. Loras eventually became a missionary to America, the founder of
Loras College in Dubuque, Iowa, and the first bishop of
the Dubuque diocese.

It takes guts to invoke a saint who was clocked by your first
bishop, and so in honor of this patronage we recommend a
classic nineteenth-century concoction called a Whiskey
Smash. We hope those sons-of-saint-smackers in Dubuque
like it.

WHISKEY SMASH

3 lemon wedges
4 mint leaves
½ oz. simple syrup

2 oz. Elijah Craig 12-year-old
bourbon
1 mint sprig

Muddle the lemon wedges in a shaker. Add mint leaves, simple syrup, bourbon, and ice and shake forty times. Double-strain into an old-fashioned glass over one large ice cube. Slap the mint sprig between your hands and use as a garnish. Serve with a straw if you wish.

PATRONAGES | The Archdiocese of Dubuqe (Iowa), priests (especially diocesan) *Suggested Patronages Dirty dancing (against), draft-dodging, Southern Baptists (whether they like it or not), taverns (against), students who struggle taking exams*

LAST CALL

A toast: "May the prayers and example of St. John Vianney sanctify and strengthen our diocesan priests and drive away any demons in their life. And may the saint help us keep our dancing within acceptable limits."

ST. JOHN THE BAPTIST, JUNE 24 (BIRTHDAY) AND AUGUST 29 (MARTYRDOM)

The "Precursor of the Lord" who abstained from all strong drink was beheaded when he spoke truth to power by preaching against King Herod's marriage. John the Baptist has taken on some odd patronages over the years. We assume that he is the patron saint of bird dealers because he is often portrayed with the Holy Spirit as a dove over his head, and we know that he became the patron saint of tailors because he made his own clothes. (God bless tailors for wanting to become his client; you would think that they would resent him for setting such an example.) John is the patron saint of shepherds and lambs because he called Jesus the Lamb of God, and believe it or not, he is the patron saint of highways and stonemasons because he makes straight the way of the Lord.

John the Baptist is also a patron saint of Puerto Rico, the national drink of which is the Piña Colada.

Piña Colada

2 oz. coconut milk
2 oz. pineapple juice
2 oz. light rum or coconut rum

1 pineapple wedge
1 maraschino cherry

Mix all liquid ingredients with two cups of ice in a blender and blend at high speed until it is smooth. Pour into a tall glass (such as a Poco Grande or a hurricane glass) and garnish with pineapple wedge and cherry.

PATRONAGES | Baptism, bird dealers, highways, Jordan, Knights Hospitaller, lambs, Puerto Rico, shepherds, spas (we're not making this up), stonemasons, tailors
Suggested Patronages *Lumbersexuals (they have the same barber) and teetotalers*

LAST CALL
"A toast to John the Baptist: may he help keep our faith and our wits about us even when we lose our heads."

ST. JOHN THE EVANGELIST, DECEMBER 27 AND MAY 6 (FEAST OF THE CHURCH OF ST. JOHN AT THE LATIN GATE)

St. John the Apostle wrote the fourth Gospel and thus came to be patron of fields related to writing. The Beloved Disciple is also a patron saint of friendships, perhaps because his Gospel contains the comforting words of Our Lord: "Greater love than this no man hath, that a man lay down his life for his friends. You are my friends, if you do the things that I command you" (John 15:13–15).

John is a patron saint of Asia Minor and Turkey because of his missionary work there. He is also the patron invoked against poison because an enemy poisoned his drink, but John neutralized the poison by blessing it. The emperor condemned John to death by having him dipped into a cauldron of boiling oil, but his biographers relate that when he emerged he looked better and stronger than when he was put in. For this reason, John is a protector against burns, and we also nominate him patron of spa days (the old feast of St. John at the Latin Gate, which commemorates the boiling, could become National Catholic Spa Day). After the failed execution, the frustrated authorities exiled John to the island of Patmos, where he wrote the Book of Revelation, portraying his old Roman buddies as the Whore of Babylon. The pen is mightier than the pot.

There is a special blessing for wine and strong drink on the feast of St. John (December 27). The blessed liquid was considered a sacramental and used in a variety of ways: it was poured into every barrel of the family wine cellar or kept in the house throughout the year for newlyweds to drink immediately after the wedding, for travelers before a trip, and for the dying after receiving Last Rites as "the last earthly drink to strengthen them for their departure from this world."[7] St. John's wine can also be mulled for a spicy hot drink on a cold winter's night.

As for a cocktail, have a Thunderclap to honor the man referred to by Our Lord as a "son of thunder" (Mark 3:17).

ST. JOHN'S WINE

1 quart red wine
½ cup sugar
3 whole cloves

2 two-inch cinnamon sticks
½ tsp. ground nutmeg
1⁄16 tsp. ground cardamom

Pour ingredients into a large saucepan and boil for five minutes. Serve hot. Makes approximately eight one-cup servings.

THUNDERCLAP

¾ oz. gin
¾ oz. rye or bourbon

1 oz. brandy

Pour ingredients into a mixing glass with ice and stir forty times. Strain into a cocktail glass.

PATRONAGES | Asia Minor, authors, burns, compositors, engravers, friendships, lithographers, papermakers, poison sufferers, poison, Turkey, typesetters
Suggested Patronage Spas

> **LAST CALL**
>
> The full blessing for St. John drinks can be found in *Drinking with the Saints*, pp. 374–75. Here is an excerpt adapted for a toast: "Through the intercession of St. John, may we be protected from every sickness of poison and from every kind of harm; and, offering ourselves up body and soul, may we be delivered from all fault."

ST. JOSEPH, MARCH 19 (SPOUSE OF THE B.V.M.) AND MAY 1 (THE WORKER)

The foster father of Our Lord and the spouse of the Blessed Virgin Mary is not just a patron saint but a *universal* patron. Consider the following: 1) Joseph is the head of the Holy Family; 2) the Holy Family is the Church *in ovo*; 3) therefore, Joseph extends to the entire Church the same tremendous love and protection that he showered on his earthly family. "Some Saints are privileged to extend to us their patronage with particular efficacy in certain needs but not in others," St. Thomas Aquinas is said to have written. "But our holy patron St. Joseph has the power to assist

us in all cases, in every necessity, in every undertaking."[8]
Numerous other saints have agreed, turning to Joseph in times
of need and never walking away disappointed.

Joseph is also the patron of several particular causes that
relate to his own eventful life, but one of his more peculiar
patronages concerns real estate. In the sixteenth century, a
convent of nuns is said to have acquired some much-needed
property by praying and burying medals of St. Joseph. The
idea caught on, although it moved from buying property to
selling it and from medals to statues. Nowadays it is customary
for home-sellers to bury a statue of the saint upside down in
the backyard: because Joseph does not like being in this position, the indignity incentivizes him to work harder. Then, once
the deal is closed, the owners dig St. Joseph up. Finally, the
statue is given a place of prominence in the sellers' new home,
rewarding the saint for a job well done. There are even "Saint
Joseph Home Selling Kits" available for purchase that include
a booklet entitled "The Underground Real Estate Agent."

A universal patron deserves the best. The Sazerac, made
from wormwood, honors Joseph's trade as a carpenter. Under
the title "the Worker," Joseph is a patron of several places,
including the Archdiocese of Anchorage. Use this as a flimsy
excuse to have a classic Alaska Cocktail.

SAZERAC

1 splash of absinthe   2 dashes Peychaud bitters
½ tsp. simple syrup   1 lemon twist
2 oz. rye whiskey

Place absinthe in a well-chilled old-fashioned glass and swirl it around, coating the inside of the glass and discarding the excess. Or, put the absinthe in a small misting bottle and spray the inside of the glass once or twice. Build the other ingredients in the glass. Note: A traditional Sazerac takes little to no ice.

ALASKA COCKTAIL

1½ oz. Old Tom gin (a sweeter, less juniper-forward gin)
½ oz. yellow Chartreuse

1 dash orange bitters
1 lemon peel

Pour liquid ingredients into a mixing glass with ice and stir forty times. Strain into a chilled champagne coupe glass, express the oil of a lemon peel over the drink, and garnish with the peel.

PATRONAGES | Austria, Belgium, Bohemia, cabinetmakers, Canada, carpenters, communism (against), confectioners, Croatia, doubters, dying, engaged couples, engineers, families, fathers, a happy and holy death (because he died in the arms of Jesus and Mary), hesitation (against), house hunters and sellers, the interior life, joiners, married couples, Mexico, missions to the Chinese, people in temporal distress (sick or lacking housing, food, or clothing), the persecuted, Peru, pioneers, the poor, purity, refugees, Russia, social workers, tradesmen, travelers, unborn children, South Vietnam, workers, the Universal Church

LAST CALL

There is a pious custom of placing a written petition under a statue of St. Joseph, but for the Little Sisters of the

Poor, notes are not enough. They place the very object they
need in front of his statue: "a potato, a lump of coal, even a
can of beer."[9] Throw a St. Joseph's party with his statue in a
prominent place. Let your guests come with their petitions
in whatever form, and then make the following toast:
"Heeding the words of Genesis, 'Go to Joseph,' let us go to
our universal patron with confidence: and may he save us
from this world's Herods, pilot us through this world's
Egypts, and equip us with what we need to make it to our
heavenly destination."

ST. JOSEPH OF ARIMATHEA, MARCH 17

A low-profile disciple of the Lord who boldly procured
His crucified body from Pontius Pilate and gave it a proper
burial, Joseph of Arimathea is understandably the patron
saint of funereal professions and roles.

Drinking suggestion: What else but an Undertaker
cocktail?

UNDERTAKER

3 oz. vanilla vodka   1 oz. crème de cacao
1 oz. Kahlúa liqueur   1 oz. chilled espresso

Pour vodka, Kahlúa, and crème de cacao into a shaker filled with
ice and shake forty times. Strain into a chilled cocktail glass, add
the chilled espresso, and stir gently.

PATRONAGES | Cemetery keepers, funeral
employees, gravediggers, pallbearers

LAST CALL

A toast to the good men and women who help us in the pious task of burying the dead, one of the seven corporal works of mercy: "Through the intercession of St. Joseph of Arimathea, may they never make a grave mistake."

St. Joseph of Cupertino, September 18

Joseph of Cupertino (1603–1663) did not have an auspicious start. He experienced ecstatic visions from childhood, but his mother treated him harshly because he was "remarkably unclever," wandering around aimlessly with his mouth agape. He also had a bad temper. And to top it all off, he failed as a shoemaker, a Franciscan (actually, they wouldn't even take him), and a Capuchin. After the Capuchins sent him packing at the age of eighteen for forgetting to do what he was told—and breaking too many of their dishes—Joseph's mother was fit to be tied, but she eventually got him accepted as a servant at a Franciscan monastery. And over time Joseph changed, growing humble and docile through rigorous penance and eventually attracting the attention of his superiors. They let him study for the priesthood, something that did not prove easy. Joseph struggled mightily with his studies, but providentially his examiner asked him about the one thing he knew fairly well, and so he passed. God worked great miracles through Joseph as a priest. He is most famous for levitating, something people saw him do over seventy times. Consequently, he has become the patron saint of flying and aviation.

Drinks: the delicious Aviation Cocktail (see the entry for St. Thérèse of Lisieux below).

PATRONAGES | Airplane pilots, air travelers, astronauts, degree candidates, flying, the mentally handicapped, students, test takers

LAST CALL
A toast: "To St. Joseph of Cupertino: even when we're not quick on the draw, may his prayers lift us safely up to the heavenly heights."

ST. JUDE, OCTOBER 28

Saint Jude, who is also called "Thaddeus" (the Brave One), was one of the original twelve apostles and probably the brother of St. James the Less. He is believed to have preached the Gospel first in Mesopotamia and then in Persia, where he was martyred. Jude is the author of a brief and strongly worded New Testament epistle that mentions, among other things, the curious detail that St. Michael the Archangel and the Devil fought over the remains of Moses (Jude 1:9).

But Jude is most famous for being the patron saint of desperate or hopeless causes, possibly because his name was so similar to that of Judas Iscariot that people wouldn't pray to the "forgotten apostle" unless all else had failed! The patronage itself is relatively recent, dating back to 1929 when a Father James Tort encouraged the devotion among his parishioners in southeast Chicago, most of whom were laid-off steelworkers. The devotion grew rapidly; on the final night of a solemn novena held on St. Jude's feast, there was an overflow crowd outside the church. The next day, the stock market crashed, and soon more Americans were turning to St. Jude during the Great Depression and World War II.

Father Tort also organized the Police Branch of the League of St. Jude in 1932; to this day Jude is the official patron of the Chicago Police Department. And because, we conjecture, many a person feels desperate or hopeless when hospitalized, Jude is also the patron of hospital workers and the hospitalized.

For Jude's popularity we can also thank a Maronite Catholic named Amos Muzyad Yaqoob Kairouz, better known as the actor and entertainer Danny Thomas. Thomas was down on his luck when he remembered how a stagehand had praised St. Jude for miraculously curing his wife of cancer. A devout Catholic who went to Sunday 6:00 a.m. Mass on his way home from performing all night in a club, Thomas prayed to St. Jude and promised him that he would do "something big" if St. Jude helped him make it big. Jude kept his end of the bargain, and so did Thomas, founding the world-famous St. Jude Children's Research Hospital in Memphis, Tennessee.

St. Jude is an everyman's saint, and for an everyman's saint, have a mixed drink like the working-class Boilermaker (beer and a shot of whiskey) or something similar to it like the Desperado #1. The Desperado #2, on the other hand, is a refined, rich, and almost smoky drink, but thanks to the Cynar artichoke liqueur it is *bitter*: be prepared for a punch in the face that will remind you of true desperation. Incidentally, like the modern devotion to St. Jude, "desperado" is an American invention (not an authentic Spanish noun).

Or you can honor St. Jude's "hometown," as Danny Thomas called the Windy City, with a classic Chicago Fizz cocktail. The reddish hue is reminiscent of St. Jude's martyrdom.

DESPERADO #1

1 beer
2 oz. tequila

1 dash lime juice

Build all ingredients in a pint glass and serve.

DESPERADO #2

2 oz. Patrón Añejo tequila
¾ oz. sweet vermouth
½ oz. amontillado sherry

¼ oz. Cynar
1 orange twist for garnish

Pour liquid ingredients into a mixing glass with ice and stir forty times. Strain into a cocktail glass and garnish with orange.

CHICAGO FIZZ

1 oz. light rum
1 oz. port
1 tbsp. fresh lemon juice
1 tsp. powdered sugar

1 egg white
sparkling water
orange or lemon peel
    (optional)

Pour liquid ingredients except sparkling water into a shaker with no ice and "dry shake" forty times to emulsify the egg white. Add ice and shake more. Strain into a highball glass over two large ice cubes, top with sparkling water, stir, and serve. Garnish with peel.

PATRONAGES | Armenia, the Chicago Police
Department, desperate or hopeless causes, hospitals
Suggested Patronage Finding a parking spot when you are
running really late

LAST CALL

Turn a popular prayer to St. Jude into a toast: "In
thanksgiving to St. Jude our patron, and may the Sacred
Heart of Jesus be adored, glorified, loved, and preserved
throughout the world now and forever."

St. Lawrence, August 10

While being slowly roasted alive on a gridiron, St. Lawrence defied his Roman tormentors by joking, "You can turn
me over. I am done on this side." As a result, St. Lawrence
has become the patron saint of comedians, cooks, and even
brewers, since the manner of his martyrdom reminded medieval beer makers of the way malt was dried. Lawrence is
also a patron of the poor because as a deacon he cared for
them; and he patronizes archivists and librarians because he
reputedly protected the Church's written documents from
the emperor.

Drink suggestion: A malty beer like a Dogfish Head Raison d'Etre, a St. Bernardus Quadrupel, or a Trappistes
Rochefort. A St. Lawrence cocktail is also a good choice: for
the patron saint of butchers, you can substitute Slaughter
House American whiskey, which has extra-soft tannin notes,
for the Canadian.

ST. LAWRENCE #1

by Victor Broggi

½ oz. Grand Marnier
1 oz. Canadian or Slaughter House American whiskey

1½ oz. sweet vermouth
1 small dash Angostura bitters

Pour ingredients into a shaker filled with ice and shake forty times. Strain into a cocktail glass.

PATRONAGES | Archivists, armories, bakers, brewers, butchers, Canada, comedians, confectioners, cooks, librarians, miners, the poor, restaurateurs, roasters, Sri Lanka, stained glass makers, tanners, vintners (probably because as deacon he was in charge of the Precious Blood during Mass)

LAST CALL

St. Lawrence's feast is a day to celebrate the sometimes macabre yet humorous aspects of Catholic life that adorn its many virtues. Why not throw a comedy or joke-telling party in honor of the saint? You can call it a Roast.

ST. LEONARD OF NOBLAC, NOVEMBER 6

Before becoming a monk and hermit, Leonard (d. 559) was a Frankish nobleman in the court of Clovis I who had permission to liberate prisoners according to his discretion. He became "Leonard of Noblac" after the king gave him some of the royal lands in that region as a token of his gratitude for Leonard's powerful prayers for the queen to deliver a male child safely. According to one legend, prisoners who prayed to St. Leonard saw their chains break before their very eyes. The saint soon found himself inundated with heavy chains and irons offered in supplication or thanksgiving (possibly the reason he is a patron of blacksmiths and coppersmiths). Leonard, in return, gave his ex-cons parcels of his land so they could make an honest living. In 1103, Prince Bohemund credited his own release from Muslim captivity to St. Leonard's heavenly intercession, and thus he also became a patron of prisoners of war.

But why is Leonard a protector against brigands, robbers, and thieves? Michael Walsh speculates that because Leonard was the fellow who sprang such troublemakers from jail, "he was responsible for their being a danger to the public!"

Drink suggestions: A Robber Cocktail, or perhaps a Swiss white wine produced by Maître de Chais called Fendant de Saint-Léonard AOC Valais.

ROBBER COCKTAIL

1¾ oz. scotch
¾ oz. sweet vermouth

1 dash aromatic bitters
1 cherry for garnish

Mix all ingredients except cherry into a shaker filled with ice and shake forty times. Strain into a cocktail glass and add cherry.

PATRONAGES | Blacksmiths, brigands, childbirth, coppersmiths, porters, prisoners, prisoners of war, robbers, thieves

LAST CALL

A toast: "May St. Leonard free us from our shackles, whatever they may be."

ST. LIDWINA, APRIL 14

Lidwina, or Lydwina, was fifteen years old when she broke a rib in an ice-skating accident. The Dutch girl's condition deteriorated significantly: a ceaseless pain in her side eventually became paralysis, blindness in one eye, sores on her face, and bleeding from her mouth, ears, and nose. (Some believe that this is one of the first documented cases of multiple sclerosis.) Bedridden for thirty-eight years, Lidwina is even said to have shed body parts such as skin, bones, and intestines, which her parents kept in a jar and that emitted an odor of sanctity. (Lidwina's mother eventually had to bury them because they attracted so much attention.) But through it all, Lidwina drew closer to Christ and even added to her sufferings through rigorous fasting. Before her death, she had gained a reputation as a holy healer of others.

We don't blame you if hearing St. Lidwina's story makes you never want to strap on a pair of skates again, but the good news is that you now have her on your side as a heavenly protectress when you hit the ice.

With skaters and skiers in mind, we recommend a Hot Brandy Toddy or the suggestions below for Mary, Our Lady of Graces, to numb one's suffering.

HOT BRANDY TODDY

½ tsp. sugar
½ oz. lemon juice
2 oz. brandy

1 lemon twist
nutmeg, to taste

Build sugar, lemon juice, and brandy in a mug or Irish coffee cup and add hot water. Stir and garnish with lemon twist and nutmeg.

PATRONAGES | The chronically ill, prolonged suffering, skaters, skiers

LAST CALL

A toast: "May the intercession of St. Lidwina keep us from the sufferings of St. Lidwina."

ST. LOUIS IX, AUGUST 25

How does a Crusader king and "the holiest and most just king who ever wore the crown" (according to Bossuet) become the patron saint of button makers, lace makers, and other rather dainty professions? Probably for the same reason that Louis IX (1214–1270) is also the patron saint of marble workers and stonemasons—namely, that when he was king of France, Louis greatly influenced all Europe by his patronage of the arts. And just as Louis was a great patron of the arts on earth, so too is he invoked as a patron in Heaven of numerous refined trades. (Perhaps this is also the reason that he is sometimes listed as a patron saint of distillers. Louis earned the reputation for being a refiner of taste, and distillation is a refinement of dilute solutions of ethanol.) The rest of the Crusader king's patronages are more or less based on his own life's story.

A High Hat Cocktail is a nice way to pay tribute to this royal and saintly patron of haberdashers. The drink is well-balanced and has a lingering finish—kind of like "hat head" marks after a hat has been removed.

HIGH HAT COCKTAIL

1½ oz. rye
½ oz. fresh lemon juice

½ oz. Cherry Heering

Pour ingredients into a shaker filled with ice and shake forty times. Strain into a cocktail glass.

PATRONAGES | Barbers, bridegrooms, builders, button makers, Crusaders, the death of children, difficult marriages, distillers, embroiderers, France, haberdashers, hairdressers, kings, lace makers, marble workers, needleworkers, parents of large families, prisoners, sculptors, stonemasons

LAST CALL

Host your own version of a royal banquet and include the following toast: "Hats off to the saintly soldier king, Louis IX. May we imitate his humble but determined crusader spirit, his tender devotion to his family, and his love of the true, the good, and the beautiful."

ST. LOUISE DE MARILLAC, MARCH 15 (MAY 9)

Louise de Marillac (1591–1660) felt drawn to the religious life at the age of fifteen but was rejected by the Capuchins, something that hit her hard. At the behest of her family, she later married and had a son. After the death of her husband, however, she and her spiritual director St. Vincent de Paul founded the Daughters of Charity, a new model of communal life that aimed at the perfect balance between contemplation and action. The Daughters of Charity were exemplary in their care of the sick, the orphaned, the mentally ill, the imprisoned, and the elderly. They were a familiar sight at battlefields; for many wounded soldiers in the Civil War, it was the first time they had ever seen a Catholic sister, and the tender care they received from these angelic nurses did much to counter anti-Catholic bigotry.

The Campari Splash has been described as the perfectly balanced cocktail. Let's wax allegorical and say that the Campari symbolizes the bitter moments in St. Louise's life, the strawberry juice the sweet joy of contemplation, and the orange juice the pulp of action.

CAMPARI SPLASH

1½ oz. Campari
3 oz. strawberry juice

1½ oz. orange juice
1 strawberry for garnish

Pour liquid ingredients into a shaker filled with ice and shake forty times. Strain into a highball glass filled with ice and garnish with strawberry.

PATRONAGES | The loss of parents, people rejected by religious orders, the sick, social workers, widows

LAST CALL

Blend action with contemplation by hosting a leisurely and low-stress cocktail party, and honor St. Louise's care for the poor by making it economical. (Donate the money you would have spent on a more expensive soirée to the needy.) Use the following toast: "To St. Louise de Marillac: through her intercession, may whatever we drink make us prone to right action, good contemplation, and a tender heart for the unfortunate."

ST. LUCY, DECEMBER 13

St. Lucy (283–304) is the virgin martyr famously portrayed holding her own eyes, which were allegedly gouged out by her pagan tormentors. We cannot list all of Lucy's numerous patronages: her association with the eyes has made her a patron not only of eye problems, opticians, and ophthalmologists, but of just about anyone who needs light to work at night, from seamstresses to writers. Lucy's name means light, and so she is also invoked in luminous trades such as stained glass and glazing. She is invoked against hemorrhages because her prayers healed her mother when she was suffering from one, and we presume that she got tagged with interceding in cases of dysentery because of its ties to hemorrhaging. Lucy is a patroness against throat infections because she was martyred by being knifed in the throat; by a certain gruesome logic, cutlers embraced her as their patroness for this reason as well. (You'd have thought that they would have turned to a saintly Iron Chef rather than a martyr with an axe to grind against knives.)

The Sancta Lucia Martini is a martini with the olives configured to look like a pair of eyes. We're confident that if Saint Lucy did not have a sense of humor on earth, she has one now by virtue of the Beatific Vision.

SANCTA LUCIA MARTINI

2 oz. gin   2 olives
1 dash vermouth

Pour liquid ingredients into a mixing glass with ice and stir forty times. Strain into a cocktail glass. Transfix the two olives with a cocktail sword so that the pimentos are positioned like eyeballs and place them horizontally on the glass rim.

PATRONAGES | Cutlers, dysentery, eye problems, glaziers, hemorrhages, ophthalmologists, opticians, peasants, saddlers, salesmen (nobody seems to know why), seamstresses, stained glass workers, throat ailments, writers

LAST CALL

Adorn your entertainment space with an abundance of lit candles and make the following toast: "May the prayers of St. Lucy light our way and save us from darkness and the shadow of death."

ST. LUKE, OCTOBER 18

The evangelist St. Luke was a physician by trade, so he is a patron of doctors, surgeons, and so forth. Because tradition credits him with painting portraits of the Blessed Virgin Mary, he is also a patron saint of artists, painters, lace makers, and the like. And because the Gospel that bears his name contains an accurate account of the life of Christ, he is the patron saint of notaries.

But why is St. Luke the patron saint of butchers? Some speculate that it is because his symbol in art is an ox (his Gospel begins with the high priest Zechariah sacrificing what we assume is an ox). Fair enough, but we also wonder if there is a somewhat unflattering comparison being drawn between surgeons and butchers.

We're not sure what real ox blood tastes like, but the Ox Blood cocktail is a swank drink with a sweet start and an orange bite for a finish.

OX BLOOD

by R. Emmerich

1 oz. cherry brandy (kirsch)	2 dashes orange bitters
1 oz. gin	3 dashes brown curaçao
1 oz. sweet vermouth	(really any curaçao is fine)

Pour ingredients into a mixing glass with ice and stir forty times. Strain into a cocktail glass and serve.

PATRONAGES | Artists, butchers, medical professions, notaries, painters, physicians, surgeons

LAST CALL

For a celebration in honor of the patron saint of butchers, make sure to put out plenty of cold cuts. After you have clogged your arteries, make the following toast: "May the physician St. Luke heal us of all our ills."

ST. MAGNUS OF FÜSSEN, SEPTEMBER 6

How does a saint become an intercessor invoked against depredating insects? St. Magnus (d. 772), a monk from the monastery of St. Gall, is credited with blessing crops with a staff inherited from St. Columbanus, thereby driving out all vermin such as snakes, caterpillars, and grasshoppers and averting all damage caused by hail and lightning. Magnus is also said to have spared an infant dragon, which went on to help farmers rid the area of pests. Today this ecologically savvy move would be called "a holistic management method of animal husbandry," although the use of dragons is no longer recommended.

On another occasion St. Magnus encountered a bear in the woods that showed him a vein of iron ore, and so he gratefully gave the bear some cake. After the bear followed Magnus to the abbey, the monks rounded up some tools and followed the bear to other sources of iron. Thus was born the area's most lucrative industry.

An obvious drink choice for tonight is that minty dessert classic from the 1920s, the Grasshopper cocktail. But you can also enjoy a Magnus scotch by Highland Park, which has been making whisky on the Orkney Islands since 1798. True, the scotch was named after Highland Park's founder, Magnus Eunson, and true, Mr. Eunson was named after St. Magnus of Orkney, one of the patron saints of Norway. But are you really going to quibble over a reason to drink scotch?

GRASSHOPPER

2 oz. cream

¾ oz. green crème de menthe

1 oz. light crème de cacao

grated nutmeg (optional)

Pour ingredients into a shaker filled with ice and shake forty times. Strain into a cocktail glass and sprinkle with nutmeg.

PATRONAGES | Caterpillars, crops, grasshoppers, hail, lightning, snakes, vermin *Suggested Patronages* Bears (for or against), prospectors, holistic management methods of animal husbandry

LAST CALL

A toast: "May St. Magnus preserve us from all fuzzy pests and creeping critters as he leads us to precious metals."

ST. MARK, APRIL 25

St. Mark the Evangelist (d. 68) has an odd assortment of patronages. He is a patron of libraries, possibly because he was the founding bishop of Alexandria, which had a renowned library; patron of notaries and lawyers because his Gospel is an accurate and concise record of Christ's life; patron of lions because the winged lion is his symbol in Christian art; and patron of Venice, which now has his relics thanks to two Venetians who stole his body from Muslim-controlled Alexandria by covering his crated remains with a layer of pork (which Islam forbids touching). Such a remarkable act of smuggling deserves a patronage of its own, and so we hereby declare that Mark should be invoked against choirinophobia, the fear of pork.

It is probably because St. Mark was dragged through the streets of Alexandria and flayed that he is invoked against scrofulous diseases, struma, and insect bites. Finally, in 1951 Pope Pius XII named St. Mark the patron saint of cattle breeders in Spain, because they asked for it.

Drink suggestion: a smooth and pleasing St. Mark cocktail.

ST. MARK

¾ oz. gin
¾ oz. dry vermouth
½ oz. cherry liqueur (Cherry Heering or similar)

½ oz. groseille (red currant) syrup or grenadine

Pour ingredients into a mixing glass with ice and stir forty times. Strain into a cocktail glass.

PATRONAGES | Egypt, insect bites, lawyers, libraries, lions, notaries, scrofulous diseases, Spanish cattle breeders, struma **Suggested Patronage** Choirinophobia

---

LAST CALL

The battle cry of the Venetians was "Piante Lione!"—Plant the Lion! A toast, then: "In the name of God, may St. Mark the Lion plant the faith firmly in our hearts and uproot all dangers to body and soul."

MARTIN DE PORRES, NOVEMBER 3

Charming stories abound about this illegitimate son of a Spanish nobleman and a freed African slave. As a mulatto, Martin (1579–1639) suffered from bigotry both in Peruvian society in general and within the Dominican Order to which he belonged; yet he rose above it to become a model of charity and a great wonder-worker. Martin healed numerous people without any attention to their rank, founded an orphanage, and gave away great amounts of food to the poor. His kindness extended even to rats and mice, which he fretted weren't getting enough to eat (we imagine that he is currently seated in Heaven far away from St. Gertrude of Nivelles, who is invoked against the furry little buggers). St. Martin even used his sister's house as a "home for wandering cats and dogs"! He never let his popularity go to his head: he referred to himself as "Brother Broom" and even once suggested that he be sold into slavery to pay for the

Dominicans' debts. When he died, bishops and noblemen vied for the honor of carrying him to his grave.

One can never go wrong with Peru's greatest contribution to the world of mixology, the Pisco Sour.

PISCO SOUR

2 oz. Peruvian pisco brandy
1 oz. lemon or lime juice
¾ oz. simple syrup

1 egg white
1 dash Angostura bitters

Pour all ingredients except bitters into a shaker filled with ice and shake forty times. Strain into an old-fashioned glass without ice and sprinkle bitters on the foamy top of the drink.

PATRONAGES | Justice, people of mixed race, public education (Peru), public health services (chiefly in Peru), racial harmony

LAST CALL

Festoon your parlor with cute images of mice, give thanks to God for society's progress in racial harmony, and implore St. Martin for his continued intercession. Do not, however, play Paul McCartney and Stevie Wonder's cloying "Ebony and Ivory" unless you need to atone for some grievous sin through extreme mortification.

THE BLESSED VIRGIN MARY

My goodness, does the holy Mother of God operate under a plethora of titles! We can't include all of them, but here are some of the highlights. If you cannot find the title you seek here, be creative and borrow from another entry: Marian titles are like different spokes of a wheel that all lead back to the same radiant center.

LAST CALL

Keep it simple and use the following as a general toast: "Hail, Mary, [insert specific title]! Pray for us and our intentions."

Mary, Our Lady of the Assumption, August 15

The assumption of the Blessed Virgin Mary body and soul into Heaven is the subject of *Drinking with the Saints*, pages 214–16. Our Lady of the Assumption has been acknowledged as the patroness of several countries because of their devotion to her under this title. In 1952 she was also declared the heavenly patron of French pilots and aircrews, presumably because images of the Assumption usually depict Mary flying through the air.

Drink suggestion: The delicious Aviation Cocktail (see the entry for Thérèse of Lisieux below).

PATRONAGES | France, French aircrews, Jamaica, New Caledonia, Paraguay, South Africa

Mary, Our Lady of Castellazzo or Our Lady of Grace and of Crete or Our Lady of the Centaurs, the second Sunday of July

Who knew that the Mother of God had a fondness for hogs? In a 1947 Apostolic Letter, Pope Pius XII eloquently describes how bikers from the foothill regions of Italy,

France, and Switzerland visit the shrine of the Madonna di Castellazzo on her feast day in the town of Castellazzo Bormida in northern Italy in order to attend Mass and receive a blessing for themselves and their rides. Afterwards, the Supreme Pontiff notes, they affix an image of Our Lady to their bikes and tear off with a great racket down ancient Roman roads. We suspect that Pius XII was having a little fun with his Latin, for instead of using the neo-Latin word for a motorcycle (*autobirota*) near the end of this letter, he concludes by declaring Mary of Castellazzo, a.k.a. Our Lady of Grace and of Crete and Our Lady of the Centaurs, the "Heavenly Patron, especially for Italy, of coachmen driving two-wheelers powered by fire-inducing liquid" (*Patrona Caelestis praecipua pro Italia raedariorum birotas ignifero latice incitas moderantium*). That's "motorcyclists" to you and me. The three-day international rally and pilgrimage to Our Lady's shrine at Castellazzo, capped by her feast day, continues to draw thousands of bikers every year.

Aperol is the most popular aperitif in Italy, and our new cocktail in honor of Our Lady of Castellazzo hits the spot after a long day on the road. The name Aperol Is Said and Done is a pun on a familiar phrase that was first used in a translation of Aesop's fable "The Tortoise and the Hare," the full statement being, "After all is said and done, more is said than done." Hopefully the bikers winding their way to and from Castellazzo are more like the tortoise than his harebrained rival.

We use Toschi's amarena cherries and cherry syrup, which come in the same one-pound can. These intensely sweet and delicious cherries are a classic topping for Italian gelato and a clear upgrade from the common maraschino found in the U.S. (you can jazz up your Old Fashioneds and other cocktails with them, too). The amarena cherry grows in Italy and is picked in July, around the time of Our Lady's feast.

Aperol Is Said and Done

1 oz. gin
1 oz. Aperol
1 tsp. Toschi amarena black
  cherry syrup

soda water
1 Toschi amarena black
  cherry

Build gin, Aperol, and cherry syrup in a highball glass and fill with ice. Top with soda water and garnish with cherry.

Another option is a classic Rossini. And for added relevance, use Asti Spumante, a sparkling white wine produced in Asti, located in the same region as Castellazzo Bormida. In medieval art the strawberry is a symbol of, among other things, Mary's fruitful virginity, because the plant flowers and fruits at the same time.

Rossini

3½ oz. Asti Spumante Brut
1½ oz. strawberry juice

strawberry

Build strawberry juice and spumante in a champagne flute. Garnish with strawberry.

PATRONAGES | Bikers and motorcyclists

LAST CALL

Here is the touching Biker's Prayer from the shrine of Our Lady of Castellazzo, which we are pleased to introduce to the English-speaking world with our own translation:

"O Madonna of the Centaurs, you who from this shrine place upon us your benevolent mantle: save us from the dangers of the road at all times and in all places. O Blessed Virgin Mary, help us so that our behavior can be an example to everyone, an example of genuine sportsmanship on the road and an example of working for brotherhood and universal harmony in our lives. Support us in our weakness and let us live as strong witnesses to the faith so that, reaching you in Paradise, we may enjoy, bless, and love your Son Jesus forever and ever. Amen."

OUR LADY OF CHARITY, SEPTEMBER 8

Our Lady of Charity is a title familiar to Catholics around the world, but her image in the National Shrine Basilica of Our Lady of Charity of El Cobre is particularly dear to the people of Cuba. According to local tradition, this statue was left by one of the first conquistadors in the Indian village of El Cobre in 1508 in gratitude for help he had received. The feast of Our Lady of Charity is the same as the Nativity of the Blessed Virgin Mary.

Whether you are Cuban or not, it is always a good idea to ask for more charity. And whether you are Cuban or not, it is always a good idea to ask for a Mojito. Cuba's most famous mixed drink is made from ingredients native to the island, and versions of it can be traced back as far as the sixteenth century.

MOJITO

2 oz. light rum
¾ oz. fresh lime juice
½ oz. simple syrup

3 mint leaves
club soda
1 mint sprig and 1 lime wheel

Lightly muddle the mint and simple syrup in a shaker. Add rum, lime juice, and ice and shake several times (no need to do our customary forty). Strain into a highball glass filled with fresh ice and top with club soda. Garnish with a mint sprig and lime wheel.

PATRONAGES | Charity, Cuba

LAST CALL

A collect from the Roman liturgy can be made into a toast: "Through the intercession of Our Lady of Charity, may God grant us an increase of faith, hope, and charity: and in order for us to obtain what He promises, may He make us love what He commands." To which you may want to add: "Charity notwithstanding, a pox upon the house of Castro!"

MARY, OUR LADY OF CONSOLATION, JUNE 20
(AND OTHER DATES)

Because the Sisters of the Most Holy Mary of Consolation looked after the elderly in Italy, in 1961 Pope St. John XXIII declared Our Lady of Consolation patron of the old and pensioners.

Console your gray hairs tonight as you toast to Our Lady with a smooth and almost painfully inoffensive Setting Sun. Or enjoy a *Drinking with Your Patron Saints* original called The Old Souls' Old Fashioned. Our secret ingredient is Fee Brothers' cardamom bitters, which utterly transform the drink (the Fee Brothers never disappoint). There is nothing new about using Old Grand-Dad bourbon to make an Old Fashioned—James Bond has one made with it in the novel *Live and Let Die*—but our choice is motivated by piety. Old Grand-Dad bourbon is named after the Basil Hayden Sr. who built the first Catholic chapel on the Kentucky frontier. It is his profile that appears on every bottle.

SETTING SUN

1½ oz. brandy
⅜ oz. pineapple juice
⅜ oz. orange curaçao (flavor-wise, any color is fine)

2 dashes grenadine
3 dashes Angostura Bitters
1 lemon twist

Pour liquid ingredients into a shaker filled with ice and shake forty times. Strain into a cocktail glass and garnish with lemon twist.

THE OLD SOULS' OLD FASHIONED

by Alexandra Foley

2 oz. Old Grand-Dad bourbon
1 sugar cube
water

1 dash Fee Brothers' cardamom bitters

Place sugar cube in an old-fashioned glass and splash bitters on it. Add a little water and muddle. Add bourbon, fill with ice, and stir. Note: for the sugar cube and water, you can substitute 1 teaspoon of simple syrup, and for an added treat you can use honey-ginger syrup (see the entry for St. Vitus below).

PATRONAGES | The elderly, old-age pensioners, senior citizens

LAST CALL

There are several toasts involving age. Here is a sampling, which we have modified in honor of Our Lady:

"Old wood to burn, old wine to drink, old friends to trust, old authors to read, and the Mother of God to console and watch over us."

"Through the patronage of Our Lady of Consolation, may you live to be a hundred years, with one extra year to repent."

"Through the wisdom of Our Lady of Consolation, may we never resist or resent growing old—a privilege denied to many."

This last toast is especially appropriate for those who use this book: "Through the mercy of Our Lady of Consolation, may the pleasures of our youth never bring us pain in old age."

MARY, OUR LADY OF COPACABANA, FEBRUARY 2; ALSO AUGUST 5

Copacabana is a territory in Bolivia, and Our Lady of Copacabana is a statue of the Blessed Virgin dressed as an Incan princess, which was made by an Indian convert in the sixteenth century. The statue was crowned Queen of Bolivia in 1925.

Because the Copacabana Cocktail is named after a beach in Brazil rather than an area of Bolivia, it contains *cachaça*, an intensely sweet and quintessentially Brazilian liqueur. We don't think Our Lady will mind.

COPACABANA COCKTAIL

1¾ oz. cachaça
1½ oz. papaya juice
¾ oz. cream

¾ oz. apple juice
¾ oz. chocolate syrup

Pour ingredients into a shaker filled with ice and shake forty times. Strain into a highball glass filled with crushed ice.

PATRONAGES | Bolivia, along with her navy and police
Suggested Patronage Discotheques

LAST CALL

Admit it. When you learned of this Marian title, you immediately heard in your mind Barry Manilow's 1978 hit "Copacabana." Feel free to sing it after the second round. Or if you are ignorant of the finer points of American pop culture history, find the song online and just try not to groove to it. Go on: we dare you.

Then, make the following toast: "To Our Lady of Copacabana: under her guidance, may music and passion be always in fashion."

MARY, OUR LADY OF GHISALLO, OCTOBER 13

In the Middle Ages, a Count Ghisallo in Italy was miraculously saved from highway robbers when he prayed to a roadside image of our Lady. Since then, the Madonna del Ghisallo has been a patroness of local travelers. On October 13, 1949, Pope Pius XII named Our Lady of Ghisallo patron saint of cyclists because of their custom of stopping to rest and pray at her chapel, located atop a steep hill. Today the chapel includes a cycling museum with an eternal flame burning in memory of deceased cyclists; Masses on Christmas Eve and All Souls' Day are said for them as well.

Fat Tire Amber Ale from New Belgium Brewing in Fort Collins, Colorado, is a good choice. For a cocktail, enjoy the very Italian Bicicletta. Not too strong in alcohol, it will keep you on your seat for that extra mile, while the bitterness of the Campari will remind you of the sensation of biking uphill.

BICICLETTA

3 oz. dry white wine (pinot grigio or sauvignon blanc)
2 oz. Campari

sparkling water
2 orange wheels (for your bicycle!)

Add wine and Campari into an old-fashioned or wine glass. Fill the glass three quarters full with ice, top with sparkling water, and stir gently. Garnish with orange wheels.

PATRONAGE | Cyclists

LAST CALL

"To Our Lady of Ghisallo and the cyclist's life: may her prayers bring us fresh air, smooth roads, and a safe return."

MARY, OUR LADY OF GRACES, JUNE 9

In 1955, Pope Pius XII declared Our Lady of Graces patroness of Italian skiers after noting the custom of skiers' paying homage to a Marian image in the town of Folgaria, Italy. Many churches and shrines around the world are dedicated to Our Lady of Grace or Graces, and this happens to be one of them.

Although a Hot Buttered Rum remains a popular choice in ski lodges and mountain bars for the après-ski, we must confess that we agree with the classic mixologist David Embury, who recommends Hot Buttered Rum for medicinal use because it promotes bodily warmth, perspiration, and sleep but goes on to remark, "How anyone can possibly consume them for pleasure is utterly beyond me."[10] Happily, in the Italian Alps, where the image of Our Lady of Graces is located, the Bombardino reigns supreme. This delicious mixed drink is made with egg liqueur such as Zabov Zabaglione, but if you can't find this Italian product stateside, use Rompope, a Mexican egg liqueur that has the added (Catholic) advantage of being invented by nuns. And for even greater pious effect, use Christian Brothers brandy. Put these all together, and you have a

Drinking with Your Patron Saints semi-original called the Snow Top Lady, which we hereby dedicate to Our Lady of Graces.

Hot Buttered Rum

2 oz. light or dark rum
2–3 oz. boiling water
1 tbsp. softened, unsalted butter
1 tbsp. packed light brown sugar

½ tsp. allspice and ground cloves
nutmeg
cinnamon stick for garnish

Add butter, brown sugar, allspice, and cloves to a mug or Irish coffee cup. Pour in rum followed by boiling water and stir forty times. Garnish with a cinnamon stick and sprinkle with nutmeg.

Snow Top Lady

3 oz. Rompope
1½ oz. Christian Brothers brandy

whipped cream
cinnamon

Heat Rompope in a small saucepan. Pour warm brandy into a mug or Irish coffee cup. When the Rompope is hot but not yet boiling, slowly pour onto the brandy. Stir forty times and top with a generous amount of whipped cream (the snow top, of course). Sprinkle with cinnamon.

PATRONAGES | Skiers, Vermont (under the title of Our Lady of Grace)

LAST CALL

"A toast to Our Lady of Graces, protectress of skiers. If it is true what they say, that skiing is a dance and the mountain always leads, may Our Lady forever be the chaperone."

OUR LADY OF GUADALUPE, DECEMBER 12

On December 9, 1531, the Blessed Virgin appeared attired as an Aztec princess to an Indian convert named Juan Diego on a hill near Mexico City. When the bishop asked for proof of the apparition's authenticity, Juan Diego went to the hill and gathered Castilian roses (which are not native to Mexico and were out of season) in his tilma, or cloak. When he unfolded his tilma before the bishop, the flowers fell to the floor, revealing on the tilma a miraculous image of Our Lady. Within twenty years, nine million native Americans converted to Catholicism, approximately the same number as left the Church in Europe because of the Protestant Reformation. Our Lady of Guadalupe is now revered as the Queen of Mexico and Empress of the Americas, Protectress of Unborn Children, and Heavenly Patroness of the Philippines (possibly because her image was raised in Spain's first formal expedition to those islands in 1564).

It is time for Mexico to yield up her spirits in honor of its august queen. Rompope is usually enjoyed around this time of year, and it has the added advantage of having been invented by Mexican nuns, daughters of Mexico who followed our Lady's example of virginity.

Or there's tequila and mezcal. The best part about drinking these uniquely Mexican spirits on this feast day is that both are made from the same plant as the fibers of Juan Diego's tilma: the agave. It's like drinking a second-class relic! For tequila, try a Mexico Pacifico, a superior alternative to the margarita.

MEXICO PACIFICO

1½ oz. tequila
½ oz. fresh lime juice

½ oz. passion fruit syrup
1 lime wheel for garnish

Pour liquid ingredients into a shaker filled with ice and shake forty times. Strain into a cocktail glass and garnish with lime.

PATRONAGES | Abortion (against), the Americas, Mexico, Philippines, unborn children *Suggested Patronages Mezcal and tequila*

LAST CALL

There is a lingering controversy about the Blessed Mother's identification of herself as Our Lady of "Guadalupe." Was she referring to Guadalupe, Spain, which has a miraculous statue of her dating back to Pope Gregory the Great, or was she giving herself a title in the Aztec Nahuatl language: "She Who Crushes the Serpent"—a reference to Genesis 3:15 and to her victory over the serpent-god adorning the Mesoamerican temples where human sacrifices commonly took place? Pray for the territories and people under Our Lady's patronage, throw back a few, and discuss.

MARY, OUR LADY OF THE IMMACULATE CONCEPTION, DECEMBER 8

The ancient doctrine, dogmatically defined by Pope Pius IX in 1954, that the Blessed Virgin Mary was conceived without original sin has inspired many to turn to Our Lady of the Immaculate Conception for heavenly intercession. In 1847 the Holy See declared Mary under the title of the Immaculate Conception to be the patroness of the United States of America in response to a request from the U.S. bishops, and in May 1942 Pope Pius XII extended this patronage specifically to American Catholic soldiers. Other countries (and a large number of U.S. dioceses) have likewise had Our Lady of the Immaculate Conception declared their patron saint.

One of our most popular drinks from *Drinking with Saint Nick*, the White Lady, takes time to prepare but is well worth the effort. For beer, turn to a Mississippi Mud Black and Tan. It may sound like an ironic choice, but in 1673 the Mississippi was named Conception River by Father Jacques Marquette, the first European to discover and map its northern portion. The French Jesuit explorer had promised Our Lady that he would dedicate the mighty river he had heard so much about to her—if he could find it.

WHITE LADY

As promoted by its faithful disciple the Reverend Robert Johansen

1 egg white	1 oz. gin
2 tsp. powdered sugar	1 oz. vodka

1 oz. Cointreau	1 dash lemon bitters (optional)
1 tbsp. fresh lemon juice	1 lemon twist

Beat the egg white and powdered sugar until firm but not stiff (a frother or hand-held mixer speeds up the process). Pour the egg mixture and all other liquid ingredients except lemon bitters into a shaker filled with ice and shake forty times. Strain into a cocktail glass and add lemon bitters and twist.

PATRONAGES | American Catholic soldiers, the Democratic Republic of Congo, Equatorial Guinea, Inner Mongolia, Philippines, South Korea, Spain, Tanzania, United States of America, upholsterers, Zaire

LAST CALL

"A toast to our American Catholic soldiers: may they put their trust in God and keep their powder dry. And through Our Lady of the Immaculate Conception, patroness of the U.S.A., may God bless America."

MARY, OUR LADY OF LORETO, DECEMBER 10

The house in which Mary was born and where the Annunciation occurred is called the Holy House of Loreto, because according to tradition angels carried the rectangular building from the Holy Land to Tersato, Dalmatia, in 1291, to Recanati, Italy, in 1294, and finally to Loreto, Italy, where it has remained ever since. Because of this celestial mode of transportation, Pope Benedict XV named Our Lady of Loreto patroness of air passengers in 1920. And because the Holy House's "walls do not rest on any foundation and yet remain solid and uninjured after so many centuries," it is an inspiration to construction workers. We are uncertain how lamp makers figure into the equation; perhaps someone can illuminate us.

Drink Suggestion: an Aviation Cocktail (see the entry for St. Thérèse of Lisieux below).

PATRONAGES | Aircrews, air travelers, builders, lamp makers

MARY, OUR LADY QUEEN OF PEACE, JULY 9 (AND OTHER DATES)

There are several independent origins of this Marian title. In 1085, an image of the Blessed Virgin Mary was erected in Toledo, Spain, and shortly thereafter peace was established with the Moors. The image subsequently became known as the Queen of Peace. Five centuries later, a French statue of Our Lady holding the Prince of Peace in one hand and an olive branch in the other came to be known as Our Lady of Peace. By 1800 that statue had come into the possession of Father Pierre Coudrin, cofounder of the Congregation of the Sacred Hearts of Jesus and Mary and the Perpetual Adoration of the Blessed Sacrament; Our Lady of Peace thus became the patroness of the Sacred Heart Fathers, as well as of Hawaii, which they evangelized. And in El Salvador in 1682, a donkey carrying a recently discovered statue of the Madonna in a box inexplicably stopped in front of the local church and refused to budge until the box was opened. When news of the marvelous discovery got around, two warring groups were so impressed that they immediately made peace with each other. That statue also features the Madonna holding a gold palm leaf in memory of the time she is said to have spared the city of San Salvador from a volcano in 1787.

Yet it was not until after World War I that "Our Lady of Peace" or "Queen of Peace" became popular enough to be added to the Litany of Loreto. Decades later, Pope St. John XXIII, in sad acknowledgement of modern warfare's tendency to inflict casualties on non-combatants, declared Mary Queen of Peace the patron of civilian war victims.

In recognition of Our Lady's patronage of Hawaii, enjoy a classic Mai Tai as you wax nostalgic about 1950s Tiki culture and the Elvis Presley movie *Blue Hawaii*.

MAI TAI

1½ oz. light rum
¾ oz. orange curaçao
¾ oz. fresh lime juice
½ oz. orgeat syrup

½ oz. dark rum
1 lime wheel
1 mint sprig

Pour all liquid ingredients except dark rum into a shaker filled with ice and shake forty times. Strain into an old-fashioned glass filled with crushed ice and float the dark rum on top. Garnish with lime wheel and mint sprig.

PATRONAGES | Civilian war victims, El Salvador, Hawaii

LAST CALL

A toast: "May almighty God, through the intercession of Our Lady, grant us the peace that the world cannot give."

MARY, OUR LADY OF THE THORNS

You've got to love Catholic logic. In 1981 the Holy See recognized Our Lady of the Thorns as the patroness of blood donors in the Province of Parma, Italy, because donors had developed a devotion to Our Lady under this title (needles and thorns: we get it). The town of Sissa in the diocese of Parma happens to have an image of Our Lady of the Thorns.

The Irish Blood Transfusion Service used to have a "Pint for a Pint" incentive program whereby blood donors would receive a free pint of Guinness to replenish their iron content (Guinness has high iron levels). Sounds like a reasonable exchange to us, so feel free to revive this custom even if you are not donating blood. Or how about a Bloody Mary? Besides the sanguinary connection, there is the theory that the British slang word "bloody" is derived from "By Our Lady."

BLOODY MARY

1½ oz. vodka
3 oz. tomato juice or, for added flavor, V8 juice
1 dash lemon juice
½ tsp. Worcestershire sauce

2 or 3 drops Tabasco sauce
salt and pepper
lemon or lime wedge, celery stick, and olives for garnish (optional)

Pour liquid ingredients into a shaker filled with ice and shake forty times. Strain into an old-fashioned or highball glass filled with ice and garnish.

PATRONAGE
Blood donors

LAST CALL
A toast: "May Our Lady of the Thorns keep our hearts pure and our blood noble."

ST. MATTHEW, SEPTEMBER 21

Before becoming one of the twelve apostles and one of the four evangelists, St. Matthew was a publican, or tax collector. Never a profession popular with the rest of society, tax collecting was particularly loathed in Matthew's day for two reasons: the taxes went to the hated Roman conquerors, and the tax collectors usually squeezed more than their fair share out of the taxpayer in order to skim off the top. But Matthew was probably an honest guy even before he became an apostle of Our Lord, and he responded to our Lord's summons to follow Him so quickly that he did not even stop to take any of his money.

Understandably, Matthew is a patron saint of accountants, bankers, customs officers, tax collectors, and the like. In 1934, the pope put security guards at banks under Matthew's protection: we suspect that during the Great Depression the Holy Father thought they could use a little extra help against desperados. But perhaps the most fitting pairing of all is that Matthew was chosen to be the sole patron of the Archdiocese of Washington, D.C., which of course includes that great magnetic center of tax collection known as our nation's capital.

The Income Tax is a vintage cocktail that was invented following the advent of a national income tax in 1913 (thank you so much, Sixteenth Amendment).

INCOME TAX

1¼ oz. gin
¾ oz. orange juice
¼ oz. dry vermouth

¼ oz. sweet vermouth
1 dash aromatic bitters

Pour ingredients into a shaker filled with ice and shake forty times. Strain into a cocktail glass.

PATRONAGES | Accountants, the Archdiocese of Washington, D.C., bankers, bookkeepers, civil servants, customs officers, financial officers, money managers, security guards, stockbrokers, tax collectors

LAST CALL

A toast: "May the intercession of St. Matthew keep our tax collectors honest and our taxes minimal. And may the revenue collected therefrom be used in conformity with God's law and for the sake of the good, the true, and the beautiful."

ST. MICHAEL, SEPTEMBER 29; THE APPARITION OF ST MICHAEL, MAY 8

The vanquisher of Lucifer, Michael the Archangel is the patron saint of numerous causes, only a few of which are listed here. Because of his successful protection of Heaven, his patronages include battle, paratroopers, police, security forces, the U.S. Air Force, and the U.S. armed forces. He is the patron saint of sailors and invoked against dangers at sea because of an ancient devotion at Mont Saint-Michel on the coast of Normandy, France. Michael, who is described in the Book of Daniel as "the great prince who standeth for the children of [God's] people," was the patron first of Israel and now of the Church; for this reason he is also said to be the guardian angel of the pope. Since ancient times Christians have turned to Michael as a patron of the sick and the dead; in the traditional Latin Requiem Mass, he is described as the holy standard-bearer who leads souls into the holy light. Consequently, he is a patron of those who transport the sick, such as EMTs and ambulance drivers. In 1941 Michael's patronage of the sick led the Holy See to choose him for patron of radiologists and radiotherapists, because radium treatments pose dangers to the health care workers who administer them. Further, in 1957 Pope Pius XII named Michael the heavenly patron of bankers, perhaps because bankers are in danger of being attacked by robbers. It may be for this reason that grocers turn to Saint Michael as well. But we haven't a clue why haberdashers and hat-makers take a shine to Michael. Could it be because he is the "head" angel?

The St. Michael's Sword is a *Drinking with the Saints* original made with blackberry brandy and Devil's Cut bourbon. According to an old Irish legend, when St. Michael cast Lucifer out of Heaven, the devil fell on a blackberry bush and cursed and spat on the blackberries, thereby rendering them sour after September 29. Consequently, folks ate blackberries on Michaelmas but not after. As for the bourbon, the "Angel's Share" is the portion of the whiskey that escapes into the air during distillation, but the "Devil's Cut" is the portion that seeps into the wood of the barrels. Jim Beam claims to have stolen this cut back from the Devil, and so we gratefully offer this portion to St. Michael.

ST. MICHAEL'S SWORD

1½ oz. Jim Beam's Devil's Cut bourbon
¾ oz. blackberry brandy

2 dashes orange bitters
1 cherry for garnish

Pour liquid ingredients into a mixing glass with ice and stir forty times. Strain into a cocktail glass. Use a cocktail spear (St. Michael's sword) to transfix the cherry (the Devil, red with shame and rage).

PATRONAGES | Ambulance drivers, bankers, battle, the Church, dangers at sea, diabolical possession, the dead, England, France, EMTs, fencing (because Michael is portrayed with a sword), Germany, grocers, haberdashers, hatmakers, Papua New Guinea, paramedics, paratroopers, police, the pope, radiologists, radiotherapists, sailors, security forces, the sick, Solomon Islands, the U.S. Air Force, the U.S. armed forces

LAST CALL

Raise a glass and say, "May St. Michael the Archangel defend us in the day of battle." Or if you are toasting the U.S.A.F. in particular, use the following: "To the men and women of the United States Air Force, who may have wings but are not always angels: may St. Michael, commander of the heavenly hosts, make up the difference for them."

ST. MONICA, MAY 4 (AUGUST 27)

St. Monica (322–387) had it rough. Her husband Patricius was a pagan who had the hottest temper of any man in the village and who cheated on her. Meanwhile her son St. Augustine joined a religious sect called Manicheanism, lived with a mistress, and fathered an illegitimate son. Through it all, Monica gave quiet but firm witness to Christ, at last winning over her husband to the faith. And she prayed ceaselessly for her son until he converted and even embraced a life of celibacy. No wonder St. Monica is the patron saint of difficult marriages and disappointing children. Having bad kids is no laughing matter, but it is kind of funny that there is a patron saint of disappointing children. When your mother tells you that she will be praying to St. Monica for you, you know that you are no longer her favorite.

There is also a story about St. Monica and drinking. When she was a little girl, Monica liked to sneak sips of wine from the cellar as she was pouring it out of the cask for the family—until a servant taunted her by calling her a "wine-bibber." Monica was stunned by the rebuke and realized that she had developed a bad habit, which she instantly quit. As an adult, Augustine writes, his mother's "soul was not a slave to wine-drinking, nor had she any love of wine to provoke her to hatred of the truth." For this reason she is a patroness of alcoholics, even though she was not a teetotaler (she and her husband owned a vineyard).

Drink Suggestions: A Merry Widow cocktail or any French wine with the AOC appellation of Vinsobres ("sober wines"). "Drink soberly" was the motto of one of the wine's greatest fans, the bishop of Vaison in 1633.

MERRY WIDOW

1¼ oz. gin
1¼ oz. dry vermouth
½ oz. Bénédictine
½ oz. absinthe

1 dash orange bitters
3 dashes lemon juice (optional)
1 lemon twist for garnish

Pour liquid ingredients into a mixing glass with ice and stir forty times. Strain into a cocktail glass and garnish with lemon twist. Note: We have found that adding a few drops of fresh lemon juice brightens the drink.

PATRONAGES | Abuse victims, alcoholism, difficult marriages, disappointing children, homemakers, mothers, wives

LAST CALL

Your homework assignment is to read book nine of the *Confessions*, where Augustine describes his mother's life and death; be sure to have a box of Kleenex on hand. Then make a toast in honor of today's saint: "To St. Monica: may she help us wine-bibbers drink soberly and triumph over domestic difficulties."

ST. NICHOLAS OF MYRA, DECEMBER 6

The man who would become Santa Claus was Nicholas, bishop of Myra (270–343). Because he helped three dowry-less maidens destined for prostitution get married, he is the patron saint of the poor, prostitutes, brides, and newlyweds. Because he helped the maidens by tossing bags of coins down their chimney, he is a patron saint of bankers, pawnbrokers, and merchants. Those three bags became the symbol for a pawn shop, and—according to one theory— because these bags were mistaken for the heads of children (was the art really that bad?), there arose the story of an innkeeper who butchered three children and pickled them in a barrel, only to have St. Nicholas reassemble and resurrect them. Because of this gruesome tale, Nicholas took on additional jobs as a patron of coopers (barrel makers), of poor boys such as bootblacks (shoe-shiners), and of repentant murderers. In France, the chagrined innkeeper of the story became St. Nick's sidekick, Père Fouettard, or "Father Whipping," who gives out lumps of coal and beatings to the naughty while Nicholas distributes gifts to the nice.

But wait: we're not done. Because Nicholas appeared in a dream to two juvenile delinquents and showed them the impact of their thieving on the lives of their victims, he is the patron saint of repentant thieves. Because he journeyed to the Holy Land in his youth and miraculously saved some sailors off the coast of Lycia, he is a patron saint of travelers, pilgrims, and those tied to the sea. Because he was imprisoned for the faith during the reign of Diocletian, Nicholas is a patron of prisoners—either that, or it was because he struck the heretic Arius at the Council of Nicaea and was imprisoned for a night before being sprung by none other than Jesus Christ and the Blessed Virgin Mary. And because to this day his relics secrete a fragrant and healing oil, he is a patron saint of oil merchants and perfumers.

Okay, we need to stop—even though we have covered only a fraction of the causes with which St. Nicholas is associated. Hands down, there is no other saint (with the exception of the Blessed Virgin Mary) with as many patronages as Nicholas of Myra. We will mention only one more because of its relevance to this book. Nicholas is a patron saint of brewers, most likely because of his association with inns and restaurants. Think of it this way: if he rescued the three pickled children in the inn, he can rescue the inn's customers when they too get pickled.

Drink Suggestions: Any Christmas ale will do, but if you are in Toledo, Ohio, check out the nanobrewery Patron Saints Brewery, since Nicholas has so many patronages. For a large group on a cold night, enjoy some hot Bishop's Wine; for smaller gatherings, turn to an Incensed Bishop by our friend Peter Kwasniewski.

BISHOP'S WINE (8–10 SERVINGS)

2 bottles of claret (or a hearty red like cabernet sauvignon or merlot)
2 oranges, quartered and studded with cloves

1 lemon, quartered and studded with cloves
15–20 whole cloves (to be used for studding the oranges and lemon)

2 cinnamon sticks
¼ tsp. mace (optional)
¼ tsp. allspice (optional)

¼ tsp. ginger (optional)
2–4 tbsp. sugar

Pour the wine into a large saucepan. Add the studded fruit and cinnamon sticks and heat slowly for fifteen minutes (do not allow to boil, as this will make the alcohol evaporate). Add the sugar and heat for a minute or two, until dissolved. Strain out the fruit and spices and serve hot.

INCENSED BISHOP

by Peter Kwasniewski

1 oz. gin
1 oz. ruby port
1 oz. sweet vermouth

2 dashes aromatic bitters
2 dashes orange bitters
1 orange twist

Pour liquid ingredients into a mixing glass and stir forty times. Strain into an old-fashioned glass with ice and garnish with orange.

PATRONAGES | Bankers, bootblacks, brewers, bridegrooms, brides, children, fishermen, innkeepers, Greece, longshoremen, maritime pilots, merchants, newlyweds, oil merchants, pawnbrokers, perfumers, the poor, prisoners, repentant murderers, restaurateurs, Russia, safe journeys, sailors, thieves, toymakers, travelers, unmarried women ***Suggested Patronages*** *Essential oils and knuckle sandwiches*

LAST CALL

Raise your glass and say, "To the real Santa Claus, scourge of heretics and champion of the poor: may he help us defend the faith and assist the needy. And may he keep straight all his patronages as well as he does his naughty-and-nice list."

Phyllis McGinley wrote a hilarious poem about Nicholas entitled "The Origin of Species," the final two stanzas of which you can work into an additional toast:

Nicholas, circa
Fourth cent. A.D.,
Died in the odor of sanctity.
But fortune changes,
Blessings pass,
And look what's happened to Nicholas.
He who had feared
The world's applause,
Now, with a beard,
Is Santa Claus.
A multiplied elf, he struts and poses,
Ringing up sales
In putty noses;
With Comet and Cupid
His constant partners,
Telling tall tales to kindergart'ners,
His halo fickle as
Wind and wave.
While dizzily Nicholas
Spins in his grave.

ST. NICHOLAS OF TOLENTINO, September 10

The Augustinian friar St. Nicholas (1246–1306) was famous for comforting and sometimes healing the dying, freeing souls from Purgatory by his prayers, extinguishing fires, and healing sick animals by giving them "St. Nicholas's bread," bread over which he had invoked the blessings of the Blessed Virgin Mary. One of the miracles attributed to St. Nicholas occurred when he was given a roasted fowl for dinner. A vegetarian, St. Nicholas made the sign of the cross over the bird, and it flew out the window.

Drink Rex Goliath wine in commemoration of the miracle involving the chicken. You can honor St. Nicholas's bread with some beer, the "liquid bread" of the Middle Ages, especially beers associated with the Augustinians, such as Van Steenberge Brewery's Augustijn line. In the U.S. it is marketed under the label St. Stefanus to avoid legal conflicts with another Augustinian community, the Augustiner brewery in Munich, which also makes beers available in the United States.

PATRONAGES

Animals, dying, fire, souls in Purgatory *Suggested Patronages*
Vegetarians stuck at a dinner meant for carnivores

LAST CALL

Ask St. Nicholas to help our friends in Purgatory as you pray that this book does not add to your own time there (and throw in a good word for the author and contributors while you're at it).

ST. PATRICK, MARCH 17

St. Patrick, the Apostle of Ireland (387–460), first came to the Emerald Isle as a slave, having been abducted from his family at the age of sixteen by Irish pirates. For six years he labored as a shepherd, viewing the time as an opportunity to be converted to Christ and to pray. He escaped and, after being ordained, answered a mystical call to return to his former home of captivity, this time as a shepherd of men. He encountered resistance from local chieftains and the Druids; was beaten, robbed, and enchained; but persevered. Before his death, Patrick baptized thousands, ordained numerous priests, and helped several noblewomen enter the religious life. He also oversaw construction of churches and taught the Irish to build arches of lime mortar instead of dry masonry, making him a patron saint of engineers.

St. Patrick is most famous for driving the snakes out of Ireland, but many other miracles are attributed to him. On one occasion he was transporting a large altar stone from the Continent to Ireland when the captain denied passage to a leper. Patrick threw his altar stone into the sea, and after it miraculously floated, he instructed the leper to sit on it. Leper and stone then cruised behind the ship for the entire journey. For this we nominate Patrick a patron of surfers and water skiers.

Patrick is also the patron saint of Nigeria because of the role that Irish missionaries played in evangelizing the country (one of our favorite buttons reads: "Kiss me, I'm Nigerian"). And we suspect that he is the patron of excluded people because of the warm reception nineteenth-century Irish immigrants were given when coming to America (with storefront signs like "No Irish Need Apply").

Drink Suggestions: Guinness, of course, or any other Irish stout such as Murphy's (which is less bitter), Porterhouse Oyster (a Dublin favorite), Beamish, and O'Hara's Celtic Stout. In the realm of ale, Smithwick's (pronounced "Smitticks") is aromatic and hoppy with a hint of coffee and barley, while Kilkenny Irish Cream Ale lives up to its name with a smooth and creamy finish. Harp Lager and Murphy's Irish Red are also fine choices.

For whiskey, there is "Irish" as they are called. Irish is not as well known as Scotch, but Jameson, Bushmills, Tullamore Dew, Connemara, Tyrconnel, and Michael Collins are all commendable. We are particularly fond of Knappogue Castle, an affordable single malt Irish (which is somewhat uncommon) and the silky-smooth Redbreast.

PATRONAGES | Engineers, excluded people, fear of snakes, Ireland, Nigeria, snakes **Suggested Patronages** Surfing and water skiing

LAST CALL

To toast the Apostle of Ireland, a simple Irish Gaelic *Sláinte!* (pronounced SLAHN-chuh), meaning "To your health," will suffice. Or how about the following:

Saint Patrick was a gentleman,
Who, through strategy and stealth,
Drove all the snakes from Ireland:
Here's a bumper to his health.
But not too many bumpers,
Lest we lose ourselves, and then
Forget the good Saint Patrick,
And see the snakes again.

ST. PEREGINE LAZIOSI, MAY 1

Peregrine Laziosi (1260–1345) began his journey to saint-hood in an interesting way: by smacking our unofficial patron saint of speedy food delivery. Peregrine belonged to an anti-papal faction in the Papal States, and when the pope sent St. Philip Benizi to talk some sense to them, the agitated eighteen-year-old heckled Philip and struck him on the face. But when Philip's only reaction was to turn and offer the other cheek, Peregrine immediately repented. From then on he avoided his worldly friends and spent hours on his knees in prayer. When the Blessed Virgin Mary told him to join Philip Benizi's order (the Servites), Peregrine obeyed and became a model priest. He was so tireless in his work that it is said that for thirty years he never sat down.

Peregrine is the patron saint of cancer and open sores—for good reason. He developed cancer in his foot or leg, and the open wound was not only excruciating for him but repulsive to everyone around. Peregrine bore this trial without complaint, and when the doctors told him they would have to amputate, he spent the night before the operation in prayer. During this vigil he went into a kind of trance and saw Jesus touch his leg. The next morning, when the doctors came to operate, they were astonished to find no trace of the disease.

Drink suggestions: Any drink with San Pellegrino mineral water, even though it is named after a different saint, the third-century bishop and martyr Peregrine of Auxerre. (See *Drinking with the Saints*, p. 110, for a recipe for a Tom Collins with San Pellegrino in it.) Or enjoy a *Drinking with Your*

Patron Saints original. Called a Leg Up in honor of Pere-grine's miraculous deliverance from cancer, it has amaretto to honor the saint's native Italy and Chartreuse, invented as an herbal elixir, to signify healing.

LEG UP

1 oz. bourbon

1 oz. amaretto

½ oz. lemon juice

½ oz. yellow Chartreuse

1 lemon twist

Pour liquid ingredients into a shaker filled with ice and shake forty times. Strain into a cocktail glass and garnish with lemon twist.

PATRONAGES | AIDS patients, cancer, open sores

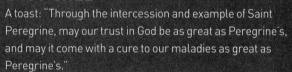

LAST CALL

A toast: "Through the intercession and example of Saint Peregrine, may our trust in God be as great as Peregrine's, and may it come with a cure to our maladies as great as Peregrine's."

SS. PETER AND PAUL, JUNE 29

The "twin" founders of the new Christian Rome, Peter and Paul are said to have been martyred in the Eternal City on the same day in AD 68. Paul was a Roman citizen who was entitled to the relatively humane execution of decapita-tion while Peter, a mere Galilean fisherman, was sentenced to be crucified. According to legend, Peter escaped jail and fled so quickly that a bandage around his leg fell off that had been covering a sore caused by his chains (we suspect that this is the reason he is the patron of foot problems—that, or because of a fossilized footprint of the saint allegedly made during the same incident). After he cleared the walls of Rome, Peter saw Jesus Christ walking towards the city. "Where are you going, my Lord?" he asked. "To be crucified again," Jesus replied. Peter realized that he was called to martyrdom and returned to face it. Feeling unworthy of dying like Our Lord, he asked to be crucified upside down (that last detail is historically accurate).

But why is Peter the patron saint of clockmakers? We suspect that it may have to do with another legend called "The Tears of St. Peter," according to which Peter arose every night at 3:00 a.m. (the hour when he betrayed Jesus on Holy Thursday night) to weep for his sin. And a clock is more reliable than a cock's crow.

Peter and Paul are the patron saints of the Archdiocese of Philadelphia, and Philadelphia's finest contribution to the world of mixology could be the Clover Club cocktail. The drink was invented around the turn of the last century for the Clover Club, a men's group that met at the Bellevue-Stratford Hotel from the 1880s to the 1920s. This refreshing and perfectly balanced drink is a feast for both the palate and the eyes, especially when served in a champagne coupe glass. And its red hue recalls the two martyrs who, although not always the best of friends in this life, became blood brothers of a higher order.

CLOVER CLUB

2 oz. gin (Oxley is recom-
    mended)
1 egg white

¾ oz. fresh lemon juice
¾ oz. raspberry syrup
2 raspberries for garnish

Mix all the ingredients into a shaker with no ice and "dry shake"
forty times to emulsify the egg. Add ice and shake for another five
to ten seconds. Strain into a chilled cocktail or champagne coupe
glass and garnish with 2 speared raspberries, in honor of the two
martyrs. Note: instead of raspberry syrup, you can muddle 3 or 4
fresh raspberries and ½ oz. simple syrup.

PATRONAGES | For both: the Archdiocese of
Philadelphia
For St. Peter: bridge builders ("Pontiff" is derived from the Latin
word for a builder of bridges), butchers (see Acts 10:31: "Arise,
Peter, kill and eat"), clockmakers, fishermen and fishmongers,
foot problems, frenzy (because he betrayed his Lord in a panic),
harvesters (Matthew 9:37: "For the harvest is great but the
labourers are few"), longevity, net makers, popes, sailors, ship
builders and shipwrights, and the universal Church
For St. Paul: Catholic Action, the Cursillo Movement, Gentile
Christians, Greece (he evangelized there), lay apostolates, Malta
(he was shipwrecked there), missions, and theologians

LAST CALL
You can turn this verse from the old Breviary hymn for
today's feast into a toast:

> These are your princes, happy Rome!
> Their precious blood clothes you, their home.
> We praise not you, but praise their worth,
> Beyond all beauty of the earth.
> To Peter and Paul: may they transform us into images of
> Christ as they transformed the old whore of Babylon into a
> faithful Christian handmaid.

St. Philip Benizi, August 23

St. Philip (1233–1285) was the superior of the Servite Order. Once, when his monks ran out of food, he prayed to the Blessed Mother. No sooner had he finished when there was a knock at the door. The monks opened the door and to their surprise found ten big baskets of bread. On another occasion, the pope sent Philip to preach in the town of Forlì, a hotbed of anti-papal sentiment. The humble mendicant was treated abusively by an eighteen-year-old whippersnapper named Peregrine Laziosi, but after seeing how meek Philip was, Peregrine repented and joined the Servites, eventually becoming a saint himself and the heavenly patron of cancer. (See the entry for St. Peregrine above.)

We have it on good authority that the meek like St. Philip shall inherit the earth. Thus a drink called TSITE (They Shall Inherit the Earth) seems appropriate to quaff while you wait for your food to arrive.

....

TSITE (They Shall Inherit the Earth)
....

¾ oz. brandy   ½ oz. Cointreau
¾ oz. lemon juice   ½ oz. Bénédictine

Pour ingredients into a shaker filled with ice and shake forty times. Strain into a cocktail glass and garnish with mint.

PATRONAGE | Florence (Italy) *Suggested Patronage*
Speedy food delivery

> **LAST CALL**
>
> A toast: "Through the prayers of St. Philip Benizi, may our kindness never fade in the face of ridicule, and may we always get our food delivered to our door in thirty minutes or less."

ST. PHILIP NERI, MAY 26

Before being ordained to the priesthood and founding the Oratorian Congregation, St. Philip Neri (1515–1595) liked to wander the streets of Rome day and night striking up conversations that would change people's lives; he even frequented the rough parts of town and persuaded several bruisers to become his disciples and, eventually, priests. Philip was also an adorably zany saint with an infectious joy. To keep himself humble, he once walked around with half his beard shaved off, and he often wore a goofy mismatch of clothes. He also skipped around like a little boy even when he was an old man, inspiring one astonished onlooker to exclaim, "Look at the old fool there!"

Once during prayer, a mystical ball of fire entered St. Philip's mouth and lodged in his chest, causing his heart to be so aflame with divine fervor that the saint had to rip open his clothes and cool himself on the stone floor. Ever after, he had heart palpitations so violent that sometimes his whole room shook. After his death, it was discovered that two of the saint's ribs were dislodged over his heart, which had expanded with the love of God.

Philip Neri was also a miracle worker. One of his spiritual disciples was a lady who confessed that she loathed visiting a certain hospital to help the sick because it was infested with roaches. Neri ordered her to return to the hospital and put the first roach that she saw in her mouth. When the dutiful woman went to the hospital with the intention of obeying his command, all the roaches had mysteriously disappeared. Astonished, she raced back and told St. Philip, who smiled at her knowingly. We therefore nominate Philip Neri the patron saint of pest control.

A "boulevardier" is a person who frequents boulevards, and we can think of no saint who haunted city streets more than Philip Neri. In fact, we hereby make him, again on our own dubious authority, the patron saint of boulevardiers and other pedestrians. And the Boulevardier cocktail, which is essentially a Negroni with whiskey instead of gin, is a drink manly enough for the Green Berets, another client of St. Philip Neri. In 2002 the United States Army Special Forces named him their patron because he "embodied the traits of the ideal Special Forces Soldier: Selfless, Superb Teacher, and Inspirational Leader." Or you can simply have any of the scotches made by Johnnie *Walker*. (Get it?)

BOULEVARDIER

1 oz. Campari
1 oz. sweet vermouth
1¼ oz. rye whiskey

1 orange twist or slice (for garnish)

Pour liquid ingredients into an old-fashioned glass filled with ice and stir forty times. Garnish with orange twist.

PATRONAGES | Green Berets (U.S. Army Special Forces), humor, joy **Suggested Patronages** *Boulevardiers, heart patients, pedestrians, pest control, and practical jokes*

LAST CALL

A toast inspired by St. Philip Neri, who used to say that a joyful heart is more easily made perfect than a downcast one: "Tonight and every night, may good cheer and Christian joy fill our hearts through his prayers and example."

After the second round, we won't blame you for wanting to burst into "The Ballad of the Green Berets." Perhaps you can have a contest for best improvised lyrics that manage to work in St. Philip Neri.

PADRE PIO, SEPTEMBER 23

One of the most popular saints in the world today, the Capuchin priest Francesco Forgione (1887–1968) is better known as Padre Pio of Pietrelcina. When he was a boy, little Francesco was having two-way conversations with Jesus, the Blessed Virgin, and his guardian angel (all of whom he could see), and he was surprised to learn that not everyone else did too.

The first priest to receive the stigmata, Padre Pio is renowned for his bilocation and miracles, his spiritual suffering, his *physical* battles with demons, and his reading of people's hearts in the confessional (making him an ideal patron of confessors). He is a patron saint of civil defense volunteers in Italy because they asked for his patronage and got it, and he is an unofficial patron of adolescents even though his enemies succeeded in 1923 in preventing him from teaching teenagers on the grounds that he was "a noxious Socrates." Strangest of all, in 2007 the Catholic Enquiry Office (a part of the Catholic Bishops' Conference of England and Wales) appointed Padre Pio patron saint of stress relief and January blues. Cardiff University had recently identified the third Monday in January as the most depressing day of the year, and the bishops responded by redesignating it as "Don't Worry, Be Happy Day" in honor of Padre Pio's advice: "Pray, hope, and don't worry." At least they didn't canonize Bobby McFerrin.

Drinking suggestions: Any beer by the Bavarian brewery Kapuziner ("Capuchin" in German) or any wine made from the Riesling or Gewürtztraminer grapes of Alsace's Clos du Capucin (a.k.a. Clos des Capuchins). Or choose from the multitude of wines produced in the Campania region of Italy, where Padre Pio's hometown of Pietrelcina is located.

A Black Devil is a nice way to celebrate Padre Pio's victory over Satan. Another good choice is a Gin and Sonic, a variation of a Gin and Tonic but with equal parts tonic and club soda. The adjustment makes the drink less sweet and unleashes the flavor of the gin, so use a gin with character like Brazos Texas Style Gin or Hendrick's. "Sonic" refers to the speed of sound, which doesn't hold a candle to Padre Pio's ability to bilocate on two different continents. Perhaps for this saint we should rename the drink the Gin and Supersonic.

BLACK DEVIL

2 oz. light rum
½ oz. sweet vermouth

1 black olive for garnish

Pour liquid ingredients into a mixing glass with ice and stir forty times. Strain into a cocktail glass. Garnish with olive.

GIN AND SONIC

1½ oz. gin
2¼ oz. club soda
2 ¼ oz. tonic water

1 slice of lemon, orange, or grapefruit for garnish

Pour liquid ingredients into a highball glass filled with ice and garnish.

PATRONAGES | Adolescents, civil defense volunteers, confessors, January blues, Pietrelcina (Italy), stress relief

> ### 🔔 LAST CALL
>
> A toast: "May Padre Pio, who promised that he would do even more for his fellow man after death, help us live up to his exhortation to pray, hope, and not worry. And may his prayers and protection drive all our devils and all our blues away."

ST. RAPHAEL, OCTOBER 24 (SEPTEMBER 29)

St. Raphael the Archangel is the patron of pharmacists and related professions as well as of eye problems and blindness, because in the Book of Tobias (or Tobit) he used gall from a fish to make an ointment that healed old Tobias from blindness. Since he accompanied Tobias Jr. on a long journey, he is the patron of travelers and the young; and since he helped arrange the match between Tobias and Sarah, he is a patron of lovers and happy meetings. Lastly, because he bound a demon that was terrorizing Sarah on her wedding night, he is invoked against diabolical obsession, mental illness, and nightmares. ("Obsession," if you recall from your Catholic school days, is when you are harassed by a demon from the outside, as was the case with Sarah; "possession" is when a demon actually takes over your body.)

A Penicillin cocktail is a fine choice for the patron saint of druggists (see the entry for St. Vitus below), but so is a Raffaello cocktail. For wine, turn to Douglas Green Wines' St. Raphael bottling or Argentina's San Rafael wines.

RAFFAELLO

½ oz. Galliano
½ oz. pisco brandy
½ oz. dry vermouth

¼ oz. Grand Marnier or triple
  sec
1 dash Angostura bitters

Pour ingredients into a shaker filled with ice and shake forty times. Strain into an old-fashioned glass filled with ice.

PATRONAGES | Blindness, diabolical obsession, eye problems, guardian angels, happy meetings, mental illness, lovers, nightmares, nurses, pharmacists, physicians, travelers, young people

LAST CALL

We have adapted toasts from two of the wedding prayers in the Book of Tobias. "Through the intercession of St. Raphael the Archangel, may the God of Abraham, and the God of Isaac, and the God of Jacob be with us and fulfill His blessing in us" (7:15). And "Through the intercession of St. Raphael the Archangel, may we see our children and our children's children, unto the third and fourth generation: and may our seed be blessed by the God of Israel, Who reigneth forever and ever" (9:9–11).

ST. RENÉ GOUPIL, SEPTEMBER 26 IN THE 1962 CALENDAR AND IN THE NEW CALENDAR IN CANADA (OCTOBER 19 IN THE NEW CALENDAR IN THE UNITED STATES)

René Goupil (1608–1642) began his missionary work in North America as a lay *donné* (a "given" or "one who has offered himself") working for the Jesuits, but shortly before his death he professed religious vows and became a Jesuit lay brother. One of the first medical workers in the tiny colony of Quebec, he joined a mission to go deep into the wild to evangelize the Huron Indians, but his party was ambushed on the way by the Hurons' bitter enemy, the Mohawks. To describe the eight weeks of sadistic torture that the Iroquois Mohawks inflicted on Goupil would induce you to drink either too much or not at all. We will mention only one: they used clam shells to saw off his thumb. St. René was finally tomahawked to death after teaching a child to make the sign of the cross, which the Mohawk thought was bad magic. He was the first of eight North American martyrs who were canonized in 1930. Saint René was appointed patron saint of anesthetists in 1951 because of his medical skills and ability to endure pain, and he is also a patron saint of Canada.

Let the Great White North provide the libations for tonight in honor of her patron. The Caesar was invented in Calgary, Alberta, in 1969. It differs from a Bloody Mary by being made with clamato juice, tomato juice with clam. Need we say more?

CAESAR

6 oz. clamato juice
1–1½ oz. vodka
2 dashes hot sauce
4 dashes Worcestershire sauce

celery salt
freshly ground pepper
lime wedge
1 crisp celery stalk

Wet the rim of an old-fashioned or highball glass with lime wedge
and dip the rim into celery salt. Add ice. Pour liquid ingredients
into a shaker filled with ice and shake forty times. Strain into a
glass and garnish with celery stalk.

PATRONAGES | Anesthetists and anesthesiologists,
Canada

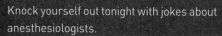

LAST CALL
Knock yourself out tonight with jokes about
anesthesiologists.

ST. ROCH, AUGUST 16

En route from France to Rome on a pilgrimage, Saint Roch
(1295–1327) helped victims of a plague, sometimes even
curing them with the sign of the cross. Eventually St. Roch
contracted the disease himself and fled to the wilderness to
die, but he was healed by a dog that brought him bread and
licked his wounds (since he is portrayed with a thigh wound,
he has become the patron saint of knee problems). There is a
legend that upon his death God promised that he who "cal-
leth meekly" to St. Roch will not be hurt by any pestilence.
Accordingly, St. Roch is often invoked against the plague,
cholera, and contagious diseases. By extension, he is the
patron of physicians and surgeons. Upon his return home in
France, Roch was arrested as a spy and thrown into prison,
where he died five years later without ever revealing his name.

To celebrate the saint from the wilderness who healed
diseases, have a restorative Desert Healer.

DESERT HEALER

1½ oz. gin
¾ oz. cherry brandy (Cherry
  Heering, for example)

2½ oz. orange juice
ginger beer

Pour all ingredients except ginger beer into a shaker filled with ice and shake forty times. Strain into a highball glass with ice and top with ginger beer.

PATRONAGES | Cattle, contagious diseases, cholera, dogs, knee problems, invalids, physicians, relief from pestilence, plague, prisoners, surgeons, tile makers (for reasons that are unclear)

St. Sebastian, January 20

The "twice-martyred" Sebastian (d. 288) was a soldier in the Roman army. He was appointed captain of the Praetorian Guard, but when the emperor Diocletian discovered that he was a Christian, he ordered Sebastian to be bound to a tree and killed with arrows. The saint was shot so many times that his biographers say he looked like a hedgehog or an urchin. Yet when a saintly widow came to bury his body, she discovered that he was alive and nursed him back to health. Undeterred, Sebastian found Diocletian and upbraided him. When the emperor recovered from his shock, he again ordered Sebastian to be executed, this time by being beaten to death with clubs. A tough saint through and through, St. Sebastian is the patron of archers, athletes, soldiers, policemen, and neighborhood watch programs. He was also invoked as a patron against the plague and contagious diseases, possibly because he is credited with posthumously stopping a plague in Rome in 680.

We recommend an Arrowhead Cocktail (see the entry for St. Giles above) or a San Sebastian. For added effect, garnish it with a cherry pierced by an arrow-shaped cocktail spear. For wine, go with a bottle from Sebastiani Vineyards and Winery in Sonoma County; San Sebastian winery in St. Augustine, Florida; or Siduri Wines' pinot noir, which is made from the grapes of Sebastiano Vineyard in the Santa Rita Hills of California. For a cold one, the Belgian brewery Sterkens makes a St. Sebastiaan Dark and a St. Sebastiaan Grand Cru.

SAN SEBASTIAN

1 oz. gin
¼ oz. rum
½ oz. grapefruit juice

¼ oz. triple sec
½ oz. lemon juice

Pour ingredients into a shaker filled with ice and shake forty times. Strain into a cocktail glass.

PATRONAGES | Archers, arrow smiths, athletes, cattle, contagious diseases, enemies of religion, lead workers, neighborhood watch, physicians, the plague, police, soldiers
Suggested Patronage Pincushions

LAST CALL
A toast: "May St. Sebastian the twice-martyred protect us from the slings and arrows of outrageous fortune."

BL. SEBASTIAN OF APARICIO, FEBRUARY 25

One of the most interesting beatified men you have never heard of is Blessed Sebastian de Aparicio y del Pardo, O.F.M. (1502–1600). A Spanish peasant who emigrated to Puebla, Mexico, in 1533, Sebastian was an outstanding entrepreneur. He cultivated indigenous maize and European wheat and was one of the first to raise cattle in Mexico. Because he obtained permission to ride out into the brush and round up wild cattle, he is considered the first cowboy, or *charro*. Recognizing the need for good infrastructure to facilitate trade, Sebastian spent ten years building a 466-mile road from Mexico City to Zacatecas, which is still in use today. Given his business acumen and work ethic, it is not surprising that Sebastian became a wealthy man. Yet he lived ascetically, gave away his money generously, shared his faith with the native population, and taught them how to use horses, oxen, and wheeled vehicles (all of which were new to them). Feeling pressure to marry, at the age of sixty he wed a young woman with no dowry (and thus no hope of finding a husband); they had a "white marriage," living as brother and sister. His bride died the next year, and Sebastian married a second time with the same arrangement and outlived his second wife as well. (Is celibacy good for men's health and bad for women's?) Finally, at the age of seventy-two, Sebastian became a lay Franciscan brother, begging alms for his community until his death at the age of ninety-seven. He performed over three hundred miracles during his life, and his body remains incorrupt to this day.

Tonight, let the bounty of Mexico honor her first *charro*. The Last Word is one of the world's most delicious cocktails. Recently it has become fashionable to swap its main ingredient, gin, with mezcal, tequila's older, smokier, and more distinguished cousin. The retooled cocktail has been variously called a Mezcal Last Word, a Closing Argument, the Oaxacan Last Word, and a Last of the Oaxacans. We have chosen the humble but reputable Monte Alban mezcal for our version and called it Me a Mexican Cowboy. The name honors Blessed Sebastian's pioneering ranching methods but also alludes to the charming anecdote about a little boy learning to serve the old Latin Mass who thought that the line in the Confiteor, "*mea culpa, mea culpa, mea maxima culpa*" ("through my fault, through my fault, through my most grievous fault"), was "me a cowboy, me a cowboy, me a Mexican cowboy." We are confident that Blessed Sebastian, who devoutly assisted at this Mass, would be amused.

Or, if you are in the mood for a spirit powerful enough to make your body either incorrupt or very corrupt, Garrison Brothers in Hye, Texas, has a rare and highly esteemed Cowboy Bourbon that weighs in at a whopping 137 proof.

ME A MEXICAN COWBOY

¾ oz. Monte Alban mezcal

¾ oz. green Chartreuse

¾ oz. maraschino liqueur

¾ oz. lime juice

Pour all ingredients in a shaker filled with ice and shake forty times. Strain into a cocktail glass.

PATRONAGES | Motorists, road builders, the transportation industry (in Mexico) **Suggested Patronage** *Cowboys*

LAST CALL

A toast: "May Blessed Sebastian of Aparicio, the world's first and holiest cowboy, keep us safe on the road and straight and tall in the saddle."

SOULS IN PURGATORY, NOVEMBER 2

You may think that we're equivocating on the meaning of "saint" by including the souls in *Purgatory* in a book on *heavenly* patrons, and in some ways you're right. But let us not forget that in Catholic parlance the souls currently being purged of their debts to God in the afterlife are called the "Holy Souls" as well as the "Poor Souls." For those souls are indeed holy. Whatever degree of holiness you have at the moment of your death is the holiness that you will have for all eternity: Purgatory does not make you holier but purges you of any residual punishment you owe for sins that have already been forgiven. The Holy Souls are glad to meet the demands of divine justice, and while they cannot pray for themselves, they can pray for us, the Church Militant here below. In other words, in addition to praying *for* the souls in Purgatory (which we should do every day) we can pray *to* them and ask for their patronage. Hey, what else are they going to do?

There's an old story that is good to remember. A fellow who faithfully prayed for the souls in Purgatory died and went to the Pearly Gates to be judged. Jesus was not terribly impressed with the man's life, and as He was contemplating where to put him among the Elect, He heard a chorus of souls in Heaven who had once been in Purgatory say with one voice, "But he prayed for us!" He got in.

When Ted Kilgore was bartender and bar manager at the Monarch Restaurant in Maplewood, Missouri, he created the mesmerizing Purgatory cocktail for an employee who had suffered "a long and rough night" and wanted something to ease the pain. Kilgore includes a warning with his recipe: "If you drink very many of these in succession, you will experience this drink's namesake. You have been forewarned."[11] We don't know Ted's religious affiliation, but his choice of Bénédictine and Chartreuse could not be more Catholic; Bénédictine is a liqueur that hearkens to the days when Benedictine monks made elixirs, and Chartreuse is still made by Carthusian monks, only two of whom know the recipe at any given time.

Note: you will want to stick with the high-proof rye to counterbalance these two strong-personality liqueurs.

PURGATORY

by Ted Kilgore

2½ oz. Rittenhouse 100 proof straight rye whiskey	¾ oz. green Chartreuse
¾ oz. Bénédictine liqueur	1 lemon wedge or twist

Pour liquid ingredients into a mixing glass with ice and stir for thirty seconds. Strain into a chilled cocktail glass and garnish with lemon.

PATRONAGE | You name it.

🔔 **LAST CALL**

How often does the perfect toast come with a partial indulgence? Yet that is precisely the case with the prayer, "Eternal rest grant unto them, O Lord, and let perpetual light shine upon them. May they rest in peace." The Church grants a partial indulgence every time it is piously said for the souls of the faithful departed. Drinking each time the prayer is said, however, is not required to attain the indulgence.

ST. THÉRÈSE OF LISIEUX, OCTOBER 3 (OCTOBER 1)

One of the most popular saints of the twentieth century, Thérèse of the Child Jesus and the Holy Face, O.C.D., (1873–1897) was a French Carmelite nun who is famous for her spirituality of "the Little Way," which she describes in terms of a shortcut or elevator to God:

> We are in a century of inventions; now one does not even have to take the trouble to climb the steps of a stairway; in the homes of the rich an elevator replaces them nicely. I, too, would like to find an elevator to lift me up to Jesus, for I am too little to climb the rough stairway of perfection.

This "elevator" consists of offering little daily sacrifices by doing "the least of actions for love." The "Little Flower," as she is known, lived this life to perfection during her brief twenty-four years and was designated a Doctor of the Church by Pope St. John Paul II.

Before she died in 1897, Thérèse promised that she would "spend my Heaven doing good on earth," and my, did she keep her word. During World War I (years before her canonization), combatants on both sides reported seeing a Carmelite nun aiding the wounded on the front lines. Consequently, many soldiers, especially the French, began carrying her image with them into battle. French pilots in particular became attached to her, and that is how she became an intercessor for aviators.

Thérèse is the patroness of tuberculosis because she died of it, and we suspect that AIDs patients were put under her care because she was associated with an incurable disease. She is an unofficial patroness of Russia, possibly because that country, especially under Soviet rule, was considered mission territory. And we needn't worry about the irony of a cloistered nun becoming patron saint of missions. Thérèse had once wanted to be a missionary to Hanoi, but even before that plan fell through, she prayed ceaselessly in her convent for the missions and corresponded with missionaries from around the world. (She was officially made a patron of the missions only two years after her canonization.) And, of course, it is easy to see why the Little Flower, who promised "a shower of roses" from Heaven, is the patroness of florists and flower growers.

The Aviation Cocktail, which celebrated its one hundredth birthday in 2016, is a classic, its crème de violette liqueur adding a luminous hint of purple.

AVIATION COCKTAIL

by Hugo Ensslin

1½ oz. gin
¾ oz. lemon juice
2 dashes maraschino liqueur

2 dashes crème de violette
(substitute: Crème Yvette)
1 cherry

Pour liquid ingredients into a shaker filled with ice and shake forty times. Strain into a cocktail glass and garnish with cherry.

PATRONAGES | AIDS patients, airplane pilots, aviation, Central Africa, florists, flower growers, foreign missions, France, missionaries, Russia, tuberculosis, the U.S. Air Force

LAST CALL

A toast to the Little Flower: "May she help us when we fly, when we grow flowers, and when we spread the Gospel. But most of all, may she help us find the express elevator to the life of virtue, holiness, and friendship wih God."

St. Thomas Aquinas, March 7 (January 28)

Thomas (1225–1274) was a Dominican priest, a professor at the University of Paris, a Doctor of the Church, and arguably the greatest theologian of all time. No wonder Pope Leo XIII made him the patron saint of Catholic educational institutions and all who pursue learning. One of Thomas's masterpieces, the *Summa Theologiae*, has some excellent reflections on the consumption of wine. For instance, in explaining that extreme abstinence is a vice, Thomas writes that "if a man were knowingly to abstain from wine to the extent of molesting nature grievously, he would not be free from sin" (*ST* II-II.150.1.ad 1). Let us be sure not to molest our nature when honoring so wise a saint.

Like many a college professor, Aquinas could be absent-minded. Once, when dining with King St. Louis IX of France, he became so lost in thought that he slammed his fist on the table and shouted, "And that will settle the Manicheans!" As the stunned dinner party went dead silent, the gracious king instructed a secretary to approach Aquinas with a notepad, lest his important insight be forgotten.

Napa Valley's Aquinas Winery is named after "the Angelic Doctor"; we especially like their cabernet sauvignon. For a cocktail, pay tribute to Aquinas's social skills (or lack thereof) with an Absinthe-Minded Martini, as modified by our discerning contributor Father Robert Johansen. The Lucid absinthe that he chose is not as sweet as others on the market, and the name "Lucid" is a perfect description of Aquinas's marvelous mind.

ABSINTHE-MINDED MARTINI

2 oz. gin
1 oz. dry vermouth
½ oz. Lucid Absinthe Supéri-
   eure

1½ oz. diluted simple syrup
1 tbsp. fresh lemon juice (½
   lemon)
1 lemon twist

To make the diluted simple syrup, take ¾ oz. regular simple syrup (equal parts sugar and water) and add ¾ oz. water. Pour ingredients into a shaker filled with ice and shake forty times. Strain into a cocktail glass.

PATRONAGES | Apologists, booksellers, colleges, scholars, schools, students, philosophers, theologians, universities

LAST CALL

Brush up on your Thomist epistemology with the following toast: "Through the intercession of St. Thomas Aquinas, may our agent intellects never lack illumination, may our senses never lack something good to drink, and may the Angelic Doctor help our schools, our teachers, and our students come to the Good, the True, and the Beautiful."

ST. THOMAS MORE, JULY 9 (JUNE 22)

When King Henry VIII divorced Catherine of Aragon and made himself head of the Church of England, Thomas More resigned his position as chancellor. An escalating persecution of More followed, ending with his martyrdom on July 6, 1535. Called by Erasmus a "man for all seasons" because he was the kind of friend you wanted in every conceivable situation, Thomas More was well known for his integrity, wit, and wisdom. Even on the gallows he kept his gentle humor, asking the executioner if he could remove his beard from the chopping block, since *it* had not been convicted of high treason.

Pope St. John Paul II declared St. Thomas More the patron saint of statesmen and politicians in 2000, and he is an obvious choice for protecting lawyers and those in related professions since, before entering civil service, he was the most successful private lawyer in England. More is a patron of adopted children and stepparents because, in addition to his four children, he took in two orphans and gave them the same love and education as his own flesh and blood.

Enjoy A Drink for All Seasons, a *Drinking with Your Patrons Saints* original. The cognac signifies More's nobility, the yellow Chartreuse (made by the Carthusians) represents his long-standing friendship with that order, and the bitters, lemon juice, and Cointreau together recall the bittersweetness of his martyrdom.

A DRINK FOR ALL SEASONS

1½ oz. cognac
½ oz. yellow Chartreuse
½ oz. Cointreau

½ oz. lemon juice
3 dashes Angostura bitters

Pour ingredients into a shaker filled with ice and shake forty times. Strain into a cocktail glass.

PATRONAGES | Adopted children, attorneys, civil servants, court clerks, lawyers, politicians, statesmen, stepparents **Suggested Patronage** Second helpings (get it?)

LAST CALL

You can toast to the merry More with an adaptation of his own last words: "To being God's good servant first and the king's second: may the prayers and example of St. Thomas More help us always keep our priorities straight."

ST. THOMAS THE APOSTLE, DECEMBER 21 (JULY 3)

The apostle famous for his doubts is hailed as the Apostle of India and Pakistan because it is believed that he spread the Gospel to those lands and founded the ancient community of "St. Thomas Christians." According to one legend, it was in India that Thomas, an experienced carpenter, was commissioned to build a palace for a local king but spent the money instead on the poor so that the monarch would have an eternal abode in Heaven. The king was not pleased with this spiritual application of his money and threw Thomas into jail. St. Thomas escaped and went on to become the heavenly patron of architects and related professions.

Thomas is also associated with beer, at least in Norway. In the Middle Ages, St. Thomas's Day on December 21 was the last day in that country to finish brewing one's Christmas ales before preparing spiritually for the Twelve Days of Christmas. The doubting apostle was nicknamed "St. Thomas the Brewer," and Norwegians would spend his feast day visiting each other's homes and sampling each other's brews.

Drink suggestions: A Norwegian beer such as Nogne or Haandbryggeriet, an India Pale Ale, or a delicious Builder Upper cocktail.

BUILDER UPPER

2 oz. lemon juice
1½ oz. cognac
1 oz. Bénédictine

soda water
1 lemon spiral

Build juice, cognac, and Bénédictine in a highball glass filled with ice. Top with soda water and garnish with lemon. Stir before drinking.

PATRONAGES | Architects, brewers, builders, doubt, geometers, India, joiners, Pakistan, stonemasons, surveyors

LAST CALL

"Through the intercession of St. Thomas, may we never tear down through doubt what shouldn't be torn down, and may we only build up through faith what should be built up."

ST. VALENTINE, FEBRUARY 14

Valentine was a priest in Rome who was martyred on this day in 270. According to one story, when he was imprisoned he wrote a letter to the jailer's daughter, signing it "your Valentine" (hence his patronage of greeting cards); according to another, the saintly priest played matchmaker for the jailer's daughter and thus is the patron of lovers. We also suspect that it is this association with lovers that explains his patronage of fainters.

But historically, the most likely reason for Valentine's patronage of romantic love is that February 14 is the day before the Roman Lupercalia, when young people would choose courtship partners for a year or propose marriage. It was only natural that once the old gods were dethroned, the Christian faith should baptize some of these harmless customs.

A Chocolate Valentine makes a great after-dinner drink.

CHOCOLATE VALENTINE

¾ oz. vanilla vodka
¾ oz. dark crème de cacao
½ oz. cherry juice

1 splash cream
1 splash soda water
1 sprig of mint

Pour ingredients into a shaker filled with ice and shake forty times. Strain into a cocktail glass and garnish with mint.

PATRONAGES | Engaged couples, fainting, greeting card manufacturers, greetings, kidney disease (not sure why, but it is often tied to heart disease), lovers

> **LAST CALL**
>
> "May almighty God, through the intercession of His holy martyr Valentine, keep our loves pure and our kidneys healthy, and may he keep us from fainting along the way."

St. Vitus, June 15

The little that is known of St. Vitus (Guy in French and Guido in Italian) has been supplemented by holy lore. A native of Sicily in the third century, he is said to have been martyred at the age of twelve by being boiled in a cauldron of oil. Before that, angels were seen dancing with him in prison. Consequently, Vitus is a patron saint of dancers (and by extension, all involved in show business, such as comedians and actors). And as one of the Fourteen Holy Helpers, he is invoked against epilepsy and other nervous disorders such as "St. Vitus' Dance" (Sydenham's chorea). He and his companions are said to have remained unharmed in a storm that killed many pagans, and so he is invoked against lightning and storms. And because he was untouched by a lion set upon him, he is invoked against animal attacks. Vitus was also known for his early rising, and so he is also the patron saint of those who have difficulty getting up in the morning—a good saint to know for those who use this book too much.

Today modern medicine recommends penicillin rather than prayer as the cure to St. Vitus' Dance, but why not have both? Honor St. Vitus with one of our favorite scotch cocktails, the Penicillin (for the dash of Islay, we recommend Laphroaig for quality or McClelland for value). Like St. Vitus, however, you'll need to get up early in the morning to make this drink properly: ideally, the honey-ginger syrup needs to steep overnight.

PENICILLIN

2 oz. blended scotch
¾ oz. fresh lemon juice
¾ oz. honey-ginger syrup

¼ oz. Islay single malt scotch
candied ginger for garnish

Pour blended scotch, lemon juice, and honey-ginger syrup into a shaker filled with ice and shake forty times. Strain into an old-fashioned glass filled with ice, top with single malt scotch, and garnish with a piece of candied ginger on a cocktail stick.

To make the honey-ginger syrup, combine 1 cup of honey, 1 six-inch piece of peeled and thinly sliced ginger, and 1 cup of water in a saucepan over high heat, and bring to a boil. Reduce heat to medium and simmer for 5 minutes. Place in the refrigerator to steep overnight and then strain with a cheesecloth. Makes at least twelve ounces, enough for sixteen servings.

PATRONAGES | Actors, animal attacks, comedians, dancers, dog attacks, epilepsy, lightning, marching auxiliaries, nervous disorders, oversleeping, snake attacks, St. Vitus' Dance, storms **Suggested Patronage** Jimmy legs (Restless legs syndrome)

LAST CALL

A toast: "May St. Vitus help us get up refreshed and early, even after a night of revelry, and may we dance only for joy and not from disease."

ST. WENCESLAUS, SEPTEMBER 28

Wenceslaus, the hero of the beloved Christmas carol, was a tenth-century duke of Bohemia who was martyred by his wicked brother while praying in church. He was kind to the poor and strict on himself, walking in the snow barefoot until his footprints warmed the ground from his bloody feet. And he protected his own. According to one story, he ordered the death penalty for anyone caught exporting Bohemian hops, making him a hero to local brewers.

Wenceslaus cultivated his own vineyard in order to provide wine for the Mass, and when he suspected that he would be killed by his brother the next day, he offered a toast with wine to St. Michael, a patron saint of the dead. A wine from California's Barefoot Cellars honors Wenceslaus's asceticism as well as his oenophilia. Or to prove that you are a freethinker, buck the current IPA trend and opt for a Czech pilsner, which one article describes as "an elegant outlier to the craft beer hype machine."[12] A century ago, pilsners were 90 percent of the beer market. And because they are only about 5 percent ABV (alcohol by volume), you can enjoy them while staying on guard against treacherous siblings.

PATRONAGES | Brewers, the Czech Republic *Suggested Patronage* Trade protectionists

LAST CALL

A toast: "May good King Wenceslaus help us care for the poor and keep our beer pure."

ST. ZENO OF VERONA, APRIL 12

Zeno (fl. fourth century) was a bishop of Verona, Italy, who was renowned for teaching young children their Catholic faith, a reputation that eventually made him patron saint of newborns and children learning to speak or walk. He is often portrayed with a fishing rod or a fish dangling from his crozier because according to tradition he liked to fish in order to provide for himself. One day he was fishing at the local river when he saw a horse-drawn cart crossing the river. The horse was acting skittish, and Zeno, sensing demonic trouble, made the sign of the cross and instantly calmed the horse down.

For drinks tonight, go with something fishy—in name, not flavor. There are a fair number of microbreweries around the world named after trout (Vermont's Trout River Brewing Company, Montana's Trout Slayer beer, Texas's Speckled Trout Stout, New Zealand's Crafty Trout, and so forth). But for a generally accessible brand, look no further than Bass ale. True, the English brewery was named after its founder William Bass in 1777 and not the fish, but how do you know that the Bass family didn't get its name from a really good day of angling?

PATRONAGES | Children learning to speak or walk, fishermen, newborn babies *Suggested Patronage Horse-whisperers*

LAST CALL

A toast: "May the calming prayers of St. Zeno make it easy for us to hold our horses and catch some fish."

ST. ZITA, APRIL 27

St. Zita, or Sitha, (1222–1272) spent forty-eight of her sixty years on earth as a domestic servant for the Fainelli family in Lucca, Italy. Initially her hard work and integrity earned her nothing but disdain, extra tasks, and beatings from her employers and fellow servants. But Zita considered her chores as assignments from God Himself, and eventually she overcame all hostility to become the head housekeeper, to whom were entrusted the keys of the estate. It is for this reason that we pray to St. Zita when we lose our keys. Pope Pius XII also declared her the heavenly protector of all female servants in 1955.

The Merry Maiden cocktail first appeared in the 1937 coronation edition of the *Café Royal Cocktail Book*, when many a maid was anything but merry as she scurried about preparing for the coronation of King George VI and Queen Elizabeth. The drink includes the intriguing liqueur kummel, made from caraway seed, cumin, and fennel.

MERRY MAIDEN

by A. R. Gower

1½ oz. gin (Seagers)
½ oz. kummel liqueur (Wolf-schmidt)

1 oz. dry vermouth
1 dash lemon juice

Pour ingredients into a shaker filled with ice and shake forty times. Strain into a cocktail glass.

PATRONAGES

Lost keys, female servants, maids, people ridiculed for their piety, waiters and waitresses

Suggested Patronage *Cinderella situations*

LAST CALL

When you lose your keys, try the following prayer, which can also be used as a toast:

Zita, Zita, if you please,
Help me find my doggone keys.

ACKNOWLEDGMENTS

In addition to my festive family and friends and the wonderful team at Regnery Publishing (especially Alex Novak), I would like to thank those who responded to an invitation on the *Drinking with the Saints* Facebook page and contributed to our whimsical suggestions for new patron saints. They include: James Cesare, Karen Frank, Kari Klaskin, Jennifer Gregory Miller, Lainey Mire, Christine Smith, Joel Sellier and his talented colleagues at the Heights School in Potomac, Maryland, and the hilarious Deacon Leon Suprenant.

My wife Alexandra and I stopped at nothing to ensure the very finest experience for our readers, testing every cocktail before recommending it. But we did not do so alone. Many thanks are owed to our collaborators, who often came together to form taste-testing panels: Leroy Huizenga, Alan Jacobs, Father Robert Johansen, Reid and Kat Makowsky, Eric and Lindsey Martin, Rob Miner, Luke Mitchell, Lewis Pearson, Beth and Marcel Richards, Richard and Hannah Russell, John Smith, Matt Walz, and Tom and Katie Ward. I would especially like to thank Andrew Anderson of Balcones Distilling, who made the Sink or Swim #2 and the

Double Down just for this book, St. Louis mixologist Ted Kilgore for permission to include his Purgatory cocktail, and Tom and Katie for their delicious Do Come Round.

Lastly, I would like to thank my daughter, Mary, and my son, James, who painstakingly compiled lists of patron saints for me. As Christie Mellor, author of *The Three-Martini Playdate*, points out, child labor is not just for the Third World.

Works Consulted

Aquinas, Thomas. *Summa Theologiae.*

Attwater, Donald, and Herbert Thurston, S.J., eds. *Butler's Lives of the Saints.* Christian Classics, 1956.

Augustine. *Confessions,* 2nd ed. Translated by F. J. Sheed. Hackett, 2006.

———. Sermon 224. Translated by Michael P. Foley.

Breviarum Romanum. Ratisbona, 1939. 4 vols.

Catholic Encyclopedia. 25 vols. New York: The Gilmary Society, 1907–1912. http://www.newadvent.org/cathen/.

CocktailDB: The Internet Cocktail Database. Accessed 2014. http://www.cocktaildb.com/index.

Craddock, Harry. *Savoy Cocktail Book.* London, 1930.

Craughwell, Thomas J. *Patron Saints: Saints for Every Member of Your Family, Every Profession, Every Ailment, Every Emergency, and Even Every Amusement.* Our Sunday Visitor, 2011.

Daiches, David. *Scotch Whiskey: Its Past and Present.* Edinburgh: Birlinn Ltd., 1995.

Degroff, Dale. *The Craft of the Cocktail.* New York: Clarkson Potter, 2002.

Embury, David A. *The Fine Art of Mixing Drinks.* New York: Mud Puddle Books, 1980.

Farmer, David Hugh. *The Oxford Dictionary of Saints,* 5th ed. Oxford University Press, 2003.

Favorite Prayers to St. Joseph. Rockford, Illinois: TAN Books, 1997.

Foley, Michael P. *Drinking with Saint Nick: Christmas Cocktails for Sinners and Saints.* Washington, D.C.: Regnery History, 2018.

———. *Drinking with the Saints: The Sinner's Guide to a Holy Happy Hour.* Washington, D.C.: Regnery History, 2015.

———. *Why Do Catholics Eat Fish on Friday? The Catholic Origin to Just about Everything.* New York: Palgrave Macmillan, 2005.

Freze, Michael, S.F.O. *Patron Saints.* Huntington, Indiana: Our Sunday Visitor, 1992.

Gordon, Harry. *Gordon's Cocktail & Food Recipes.* New York: Bloomsbury, 1934.

Graham, Colleen. About.com Cocktails. http://cocktails.about.com/.

Guéranger, Prosper, O.S.B. *The Liturgical Year.* Translated by Dom Laurence Shepherd, O.S.B. 15 vols. Great Falls, Montana: St. Bonaventure Publications, 2000.

Henriques, E. Frank. *The Signet Encyclopedia of Whiskey, Brandy, & All Other Spirits.* New York: Signet Library, 1979.

The Holy Bible [Douay-Rheims translation]. Baltimore: John Murphy Co., 1914.

Huizenga, Lee S. "St. George, the Patron Saint of Lepers," *International Journal of Leprosy* (1935), 337–38.

Husenbeth, Rev. F. C., ed. *Butler's Lives of the Fathers, Martyrs, and Other Saints.* Great Falls, Montana: St. Bonaventure Publications, 1997.

Jackson, Michael. *Michael Jackson's Complete Guide,* 4th ed. Philadelphia: Running Press, 1999.

———. *The New World Guide to Beer.* Philadelphia: Courage Books, 1988.

Johnson, Martin. "Pilsners Are an Elegant Outlier to the Craft Beer Hype Machine," VinePair, July 15, 2019. https://vinepair.com/articles/pilsners-craft-beer-trend/, retrieved November 15, 2019.

Kozub, Cathy. "It's a Texas Cowboy Margarita, Y'all," *Texas Hill Country*, June 16, 2016, https://texashillcountry.com/cowboy-margarita/.

Lefebvre, Gaspar Lefebvre, ed. *Saint Andrew Daily Missal*. St. Paul, Minnesota: E. M. Lohmann Co., 1952.

Lichine, Alexis. *Alexis Lichine's New Encyclopedia of Wines & Spirits*. New York: Alfred A. Knopf, 1985.

MacNeil, Karen. *The Wine Bible*. New York: Workman Publishing, 2001.

Marinacci, Barbara and Rudy. *California's Spanish Place-Names: What They Mean and How They Got There*. Houston, Texas: Gulf Publishing Co., 1997.

McGinley, Phyllis. "The Origin of Species," in *Merry Christmas, Happy New Year*. New York: Viking Press, 1958.

McGuire, E. B. *Irish Whiskey: A History of Distilling, the Spirit Trade and Excise Controls in Ireland*. New York: Barnes and Noble, 1973.

Morris, Ashley. "Cheers: Shake Up This Cocktail If You Miss the Old Swing Bridge," Star News Online, March 26, 2019. https://www.starnewsonline.com/foodanddining/20190326/cheers-shake-up-this-cocktail-if-you-miss-old-swing-bridge.

Motoclub Madonnina dei Centauri Internazionale. http://www.mcmadonnina.it/index.php?page=home&lang=it.

Newland, Mary Reed. *The Saint Book*. New York: Seabury Press, 1979.

O'Connell, J. B., ed. *The Roman Martyrology*. Westminster, Maryland: The Newman Press, 1962.

"Origine del culto alla Madonna di Castellazzo," website for the Diocese of Alessandria, Italy. http://www.diocesialessandria.it/public/document/Madonna%20della%20creta.pdf.

Osburn, Christopher. "How 15 Scotch Whiskies Got Their Names." Mental Floss, May 27, 2015. http://mentalfloss.com/article/64225/how-15-scotch-whiskies-got-their-names.

Oxford English Dictionary, 2nd ed. Available online at http://dictionary.oed.com/entrance.dtl.

Percy, Walker. "Bourbon," in *Signposts in a Strange Land*. Picador, (2000), 102–7.

Pius XII, Apostolic Letter, 11 February 1947, in *AAS* 39, vol. 14, series 2 (1947).

Powell, Fred. *The Bartender's Standard Manual*. New York: Wings Books, 1971.

The Raccolta. New York: Benziger Brothers, 1957.

Regan, Gary, and Mardee Haidin. *The Bourbon Companion*. Philadelphia: Running Press, 1998.

Regan, Gaz. "Heaven? Almost—It's a Purgatory Cocktail." SFGate, August 30, 2007. https://www.sfgate.com/wine/article/Heaven-Almost-it-s-a-Purgatory-cocktail-2523985.php.

Rituale Romanum. Rome: Desclee, 1943.

Robinson, Jancis. *The Oxford Companion to Wine*, 2nd ed. Oxford: Oxford University Press, 1999.

"Saint Patrick, the Patron Saint of Engineers." *Engineer's Journal*. March 16, 2017. http://www.engineersjournal.ie/2017/03/16/st-patrick-patron-saint-engineers/.

"Sint-Gummarus." https://www.visitlier.be/en/see/statues/sint-gummarus.

"Swinging Kilts and Flying Saltires for St Andrew's Day in Scotland." Magical Europe, November 29, 2016. https://magical-europe.com/2016/11/29/swinging-kilts-and-flying-saltires-for-st-andrews-day-in-scotland/.

Sutcliffe, Serena. *André Simon's Wineries of the World*, 2nd ed. New York: McGraw-Hill, 1981.

Tarling, W. J. *Café Royal Cocktail Book*. London: Pall Mall, 1937.

Trapp, Maria Augusta. *Around the Year with the Trapp Family*. New York: Pantheon, 1955.

United Kingdom Bartenders' Guild. *Approved Cocktails*. London: Pall Mall, 1937.

Vitz, Evelyn Birge. *A Continual Feast: A Cookbook to Celebrate the Joys of Family and Faith Throughout the Christian Year.* San Francisco: Ignatius Press, 1985

Walsh, Michael, ed. *Butler's Lives of the Saints.* Burns and Oates, 1987.

Waugh, Evelyn. *Helena: A Novel.* London: Chapman and Hall, 1950.

Weiser, Francis X., S.J. *The Handbook of Christians Feasts and Customs.* New York: Harcourt, Brace, and Co., 1958.

Notes

1. Augustine, *Confessions*, 2nd ed., trans. F. J. Sheed (Indianapolis: Hackett, 2006), 210.
2. Harry Craddock, *Savoy Cocktail Book* (London, 1930), 149.
3. Walker Percy, "Bourbon," in *Signposts in a Strange Land* (Picador, 2000), 107.
4. "St. Gummarus, or Gommaire (c. AD 774)," in *Butler's Lives of the Saints*, 4 vols, ed. Herbert Thurston, S.J., and Donald Attwater (Christians Classics, 1956), 87.
5. Evelyn Waugh, *Helena: A Novel* (London: Chapman and Hall, 1950), 205–6.
6. Mary Reed Newland, *The Saint Book* (New York: Seabury Press, 1979), 126.
7. Francis X. Weiser, S.J., *The Handbook of Christian Feasts and Customs* (New York: Harcourt, Brace, and Co., 1958), 130.
8. *Favorite Prayers to St. Joseph* (Rockford, Illinois: TAN Books, 1997), 6.
9. Ibid., 70.
10. David A. Embury, *The Fine Art of Mixing Drinks* (New York: Mud Puddle Books, 2008), 341.
11. Gaz Regan, "Heaven? Almost—It's a Purgatory Cocktail," SFGate, August 30, 2007, https://www.sfgate.com/wine/article/Heaven-Almost-it-s-a-Purgatory-cocktail-2523985.php.
12. Martin Johnson, "Pilsners Are an Elegant Outlier to the Craft Beer Hype Machine," VinePair, July 15, 2019, https://vinepair.com/articles/pilsners-craft-beer-trend/.

INDEX OF BEVERAGES